SpringerBriefs in Criminology

Policing

Series Editors

M.R. Haberfeld
City University of New York
John Jay College of Criminal Justice
New York, NY, USA

SpringerBriefs in Criminology present concise summaries of cutting edge research across the fields of Criminology and Criminal Justice. It publishes small but impactful volumes of between 50-125 pages, with a clearly defined focus. The series covers a broad range of Criminology research from experimental design and methods, to brief reports and regional studies, to policy-related applications.

The scope of the series spans the whole field of Criminology and Criminal Justice, with an aim to be on the leading edge and continue to advance research. The series will be international and cross-disciplinary, including a broad array of topics, including juvenile delinquency, policing, crime prevention, terrorism research, crime and place, quantitative methods, experimental research in criminology, research design and analysis, forensic science, crime prevention, victimology, criminal justice systems, psychology of law, and explanations for criminal behavior.

SpringerBriefs in Criminology will be of interest to a broad range of researchers and practitioners working in Criminology and Criminal Justice Research and in related academic fields such as Sociology, Psychology, Public Health, Economics and Political Science.

More information about this series at http://www.springer.com/series/11179

Georgios Leventakis • M. R. Haberfeld
Editors

Community-Oriented Policing and Technological Innovations

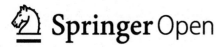 Springer Open

Editors
Georgios Leventakis
Senior Advisor – European Projects
Center for Security Studies – KEMEA
Hellenic Ministry of Interior – Public Order
Sector
Athens, Greece

M. R. Haberfeld
City University of New York
John Jay College of Criminal Justice
New York, NY, USA

ISSN 2192-8533   ISSN 2192-8541   (electronic)
SpringerBriefs in Criminology
ISSN 2194-6213   ISSN 2194-6221   (electronic)
SpringerBriefs in Policing
ISBN 978-3-319-89293-1   ISBN 978-3-319-89294-8   (eBook)
https://doi.org/10.1007/978-3-319-89294-8

Library of Congress Control Number: 2018940541

Printed on acid-free paper

This Springer imprint is published by the registered company Springer International Publishing AG part of Springer Nature.
The registered company address is: Gewerbestrasse 11, 6330 Cham, Switzerland

Acknowledgment

The work presented in this Brief received funding from the European Commission, under the:

- FP7-Security Topic SEC-2013-1.6-4 – Information Exploitation/Integration Project entitled **VALCRI** (Visual Analytics for Sense-Making in Criminal Intelligence Analysis) under grant agreement number FP7-IP-608142.
- "Ethical/Societal Dimension Topic H2020-fct-14-2014: TOPIC Enhancing cooperation between law enforcement agencies and citizens – Community policing" entitled **TRILLION** (Trusted, Citizen – LEA collaboration over sOcial Networks) under grant agreement number 653256.
- "H2020-FCT-2014 Ethical/Societal Dimension Topic 2: Enhancing cooperation between law enforcement agencies and citizens – Community policing" call entitled **INSPEC^{2}T** (Inspiring CitizeNS Participation for Enhanced Community PoliCing AcTions) under grant agreement number 653749.
- "Societal Challenge: Safeguarding Secure Societies" Topic H2020-FCT-2014-2015/ H2020-FCT-2014: TOPIC "Ethical/Societal Dimension Topic 2: Enhancing cooperation between law enforcement agencies and citizens – Community policing" entitled **CITYCOP** (Citizen Interaction Technologies yield community policing) under grant agreement number 653811.
- "Societal Challenge: Safeguarding Secure Societies" Topic H2020-FCT-2014-2015/ H2020-FCT-2014: TOPIC "Ethical/Societal Dimension Topic 2: Enhancing cooperation between law enforcement agencies and citizens – Community policing" entitled **UNITY** under grant agreement number 653729.
- "Societal Challenge: Safeguarding Secure Societies" Topic H2020-FCT-2014-2015/ H2020-FCT-2014: TOPIC "Ethical/Societal Dimension Topic 2: Enhancing cooperation between law enforcement agencies and citizens – Community policing" entitled **ICT4COP** (Community-Based Policing and Post-Conflict Police Reform) under grant agreement number 653909.
- H2020 Secure Societies Topic FCT-10-2014: TOPIC Urban security topic 1: Innovative solutions to counter security challenges connected with large urban

environment entitled **City.Risks** (Avoiding and Mitigating Safety Risks in Urban Environments) under grant agreement number 653747.
- Call for proposals 2015 for prevention and preparedness projects in the field of civil protection and marine pollution Topic: Prevention entitled **PREDICATE** (Preventing Disasters by Capitalizing on unmanned aerial systems techno) under grant agreement number ECHO/SUB/2015/713851/PREV29.
- Call H2020-DRS-2014, Topic DRS-19-2014, "Communication technologies and interoperability, topic 2: Next generation emergency services," entitled **NEXES** (NEXt generation Emergency Services), under grant agreement number 653337.

We also thank the following people for their great contributions to the success of this publication starting with the KEMEA member, Mr. Panayiotis Papanikolaou, whose technological and organization skills have no match; Katherine Chabalko from Springer whose vision for progressive information sharing has no bounds; and last but not least, Mr. Joseph Quatela, our production manager, whose dedication and assistance are unparalleled.

Georgios Leventakis
M. R. Haberfeld

Contents

About the Editors

Georgios Leventakis is a qualified Security Expert. He holds a PhD in the area of risk assessment modeling in critical infrastructure (CI) protection, an MBA, and an MSc in risk management. He has 22 years of professional experience in the public sector, of which 16 years are in security management. He has participated in several national, European, and international projects and initiatives regarding physical security of critical infrastructures, border management (land and sea border surveillance), and civil protection/homeland security technology and operations. He has also participated in tender procedures for complex security systems, including command and control and decision support systems.

His research interests include social media platforms in community policing, risk assessment modeling in CI protection, smart borders applications and tools, and integrated border management solutions. Since 2006, he was the scientific coordinator of the Center for Security Studies – the Scientific, Advisory and Research Center of the Hellenic Ministry of Interior (KEMEA) – and participated in various European programs funded by the European Commission. He has participated as senior researcher in more than 45 EU research projects, has authored several academic papers published in relevant journals, and has presented them at academic conferences.

Dr. Leventakis has worked and collaborated with many public safety and security agencies in Greece and abroad: from the planning phase of the Security Program for the ATHENS 2004 Olympic Games till more recently on the design and development of National Table Top and Operational Readiness Exercises. He has been involved in the development of **threat assessment and vulnerability assessment studies, operational security plans and emergency response plans, and procedures for the protection of vital infrastructures and governmental buildings in Greece and EU.** He has clearance to handle classified documents up to "Top Secret" level.

M. R. Haberfeld is a Professor of Police Science in the Department of Law, Police Science and Criminal Justice Administration at John Jay College of Criminal Justice, New York City. She holds a PhD in Criminal Justice from City University of New York, two Master degrees (one from CUNY and one from the Hebrew University) and two Bachelor of Arts Degrees from the Hebrew University in Jerusalem. She was born in Poland and immigrated to Israel as a teenager. She served in the Israeli Defense Forces in a counterterrorist unit and left the army at the rank of a sergeant. Prior to coming to United States, she served in the Israel National Police and left the force at the rank of lieutenant. She also worked as a special consultant for the US Drug Enforcement Administration in the New York Field Office.

She has conducted research in the areas of public and private law enforcement, police integrity, counter-terrorism, and white-collar crime in the United States, Eastern and Western Europe, and Israel. In addition to her research, she has also provided leadership and counterterrorist training to a number of police agencies and military units across the United States and a number of countries around the world. Since 2001, she has been involved in developing, coordinating, and teaching in a special educational program at John Jay College designed, exclusively, for the sworn members of the New York City Police Department. She has recently developed an online Certificate for Law Enforcement Leadership offered by the John Jay College.

Her publications include numerous authored, coauthored, and coedited books, chapters, and briefs. Among them, three books are on terrorism-related issues: *A New Understanding of Terrorism* (coedited, 2010), *Modern Piracy and Maritime Terrorism* (coedited, 2012), and *Terrorism Within Comparative International Context* (coauthored, 2009). Her other books include *Russian Organized Corruption Networks and Their International Trajectories* (coauthored, 2011), *Critical Issues in Police Training* (2013; 2018), *Police Organization and Training: Innovations in Research and Practice* (coedited, 2011), *Police Leadership: Organizational and Managerial Decision Making Process* (2012), *Policing Muslim Communities* (coauthored, 2012), *Match-Fixing in International Sports* (coedited, 2013), *Introduction to Policing: The Pillar of Democracy* (coauthored, 2014, 2017), and *Measuring Police Integrity across the World* (coedited, 2015). She is also an editor of Springer Briefs in Policing.

Contributors

Simon Attfield Middlesex University, London, UK

Clara Ayora Treelogic. S.L., Madrid, Spain

Liz Bacon Computing and Information Systems, University of Greenwich, London, UK

Raymond Binnendijk CGI Group Inc., Rotterdam, The Netherlands

José F. de Queiroz Neto CRAb – Computer Graphics, Virtual Reality and Animation, Computer Science Department, Federal University of Ceará, Fortaleza, Brazil

David S. Ebert VACCINE – Visual Analytics for Command, Control and Interoperability Environments, Potter Engineering Center, Purdue University, West Lafayette, IN, USA

George Eftychidis Centre for Security Studies, Athens, Greece

Alexander Engström Department of Criminology, Malmö University, Malmö, Sweden

Jaishankar Ganapathy Norwegian Police University College, Oslo, Norway

Ilias Gialampoukidis Information Technologies Institute, Centre for Research and Technology Hellas Thermi-Thessaloniki, Thermi, Greece

Sven Giesselbach Fraunhofer Institute for Intelligent Analysis and Information Systems, Sankt Augustin, Germany

Ilias Gkotsis Centre for Security Studies, Athens, Greece

Celeste Groenewald Middlesex University, London, UK

Junayed Islam Interaction Design Centre, Middlesex University, London, UK

George Kalpakis Information Technologies Institute, Centre for Research and Technology Hellas Thermi-Thessaloniki, Thermi, Greece

Birgit Kirsch Fraunhofer Institute for Intelligent Analysis and Information Systems, Sankt Augustin, Germany

David Knodt Fraunhofer Institute for Intelligent Analysis and Information Systems, Sankt Augustin, Germany

Neesha Kodagoda Middlesex University, London, UK

George Kokkinis KEMEA – Center for Security Studies, Athens, Greece

Panayiotis Kolios KIOS Research Center, University of Cyprus, Nicosia, Cyprus

Ioannis Kompatsiaris Information Technologies Institute, Centre for Research and Technology Hellas Thermi-Thessaloniki, Thermi, Greece

Karl Kronkvist Department of Criminology, Malmö University, Malmö, Sweden

Ernesto La Mattina Engineering Ingegneria Informatica, Rome, Italy

George Leventakis KEMEA – Center for Security Studies, Athens, Greece

Georgios Loukas Computing and Information Systems, University of Greenwich, London, UK

Lachlan Mackinnon Computing and Information Systems, University of Greenwich, London, UK

Natasha Newton Rinicom Ltd, Lancaster, UK

Ajmal Nimruzi ICT4COP Project led, Norwegian University of Life Sciences, Ås, Norway

Ingrid L. P. Nyborg Department of International Environment and Development Studies, Norwegian University of Life Sciences, Ås, Norway

Symeon Papadopoulos Information Technologies Institute, Centre for Research and Technology Hellas Thermi-Thessaloniki, Thermi, Greece

Peter Passmore Middlesex University, London, UK

Charalampos Z. Patrikakis Electronics Engineering Department, University of West Attica, Egaleo, Greece

Costas Peleties Cyprus Civil Defence, Nicosia, Cyprus

Eltjo Poort CGI Group Inc., Rotterdam, The Netherlands

Elisabeth Quercia Engineering Ingegneria Informatica, Rome, Italy

Stefan Rüping Fraunhofer Institute for Intelligent Analysis and Information Systems, Sankt Augustin, Germany

Gohar Sargsyan CGI Group Inc., Rotterdam, The Netherlands

Silvio Sorace Engineering Ingegneria Informatica, Rome, Italy

Chittayong Surakitbanharn VACCINE – Visual Analytics for Command, Control and Interoperability Environments, Potter Engineering Center, Purdue University, West Lafayette, IN, USA

Theodora Tsikrika Information Technologies Institute, Centre for Research and Technology Hellas Thermi-Thessaloniki, Thermi, Greece

Stefanos Vrochidis Information Technologies Institute, Centre for Research and Technology Hellas Thermi-Thessaloniki, Thermi, Greece

Guizhen Wang VACCINE – Visual Analytics for Command, Control and Interoperability Environments, Potter Engineering Center, Purdue University, West Lafayette, IN, USA

B. L. William Wong Interaction Design Centre, Middlesex University, London, UK

Kai Xu Department of Computer Science, Middlesex University, London, UK

Chapter 1
Serious Games: An Attractive Approach to Improve Awareness

Silvio Sorace, Elisabeth Quercia, Ernesto La Mattina,
Charalampos Z. Patrikakis, Liz Bacon, Georgios Loukas,
and Lachlan Mackinnon

Introduction

Community policing started in the United States in the second half of the century when the rise of social disorder and crime rates was so high that LEAs had to rethink about the efficiency of their relationship with citizens and about the crime-fighting model in place (Crime Stoppers International 2017). The need for a new police model involved also in Europe. Recognizing that police can rarely solve public safety problems on their own, community policing encourages interactive partnerships with relevant stakeholders. Its philosophy influences the way that departments are organized and managed (personnel and technologies), encouraging the application of modern management practices for efficiency and effectiveness. These changes can be enabled by Serious games as a form of learning. Serious games generally aim to teach or train by realistically simulating some aspect of a real-world situation and allowing learners to explore in a manner that is highly interactive. In community policing, they can be used to assist training of LEAs and citizens in the uptake of technologies, such as mobile and web applications, and raise citizen awareness about the opportunities offered in community policing mechanisms and fostering citizen engagement.

S. Sorace (✉) · E. Quercia · E. La Mattina
Engineering Ingegneria Informatica, Rome, Italy
e-mail: silvio.sorace@eng.it; elisabeth.quercia@eng.it; ernesto.lamattina@eng.it

C. Z. Patrikakis
Electronics Engineering Department, University of West Attica, Egaleo, Greece
e-mail: bpatr@puas.gr

L. Bacon · G. Loukas · L. Mackinnon
Computing and Information Systems, University of Greenwich, London, UK
e-mail: e.bacon@gre.ac.uk; g.loukas@gre.ac.uk; l.mackinnon@gre.ac.uk

© The Author(s) 2018
G. Leventakis, M. R. Haberfeld (eds.), *Community-Oriented Policing
and Technological Innovations*, SpringerBriefs in Criminology,
https://doi.org/10.1007/978-3-319-89294-8_1

1

Community policing comprises three key components: Community Partnerships (collaborative partnerships between law enforcement agencies and citizens to address solutions to concrete, and sometimes urgent, urban security problems and increase trust in police); Organizational Transformation (the alignment of organizational management, structures, personnel, and information systems to support community partnerships); Problem Solving (the proactive and systematic examination and evaluation of the identified problems for addressing effective responses) (COPS – U.S. Department of Justice 2014). Serious games can therefore serve all three by supporting training of police academies, local police, municipalities and citizens. This paper presents their use in the context of the scenarios defined for the TRILLION (Patrikakis et al. 2017) (TRusted, CItizen – LEA coILaboratIon over sOcial Networks) project in five European cities (Lisbon, York, Ancona, Lecce and Eindhoven), which differ in terms of demographics, geography, culture and primary security threats. The training for citizens and for LEAs is outlined, highlighting their differences and the approach taken to provide practical games supporting the introduction of a community policing platform to citizens and officers.

The Future of Law Enforcement

Community policing has evolved into the preeminent reform goal in modern policing, which differs from traditional policing via a shift towards more citizen involvement, geographic focus, more opportunities for interaction with citizens, and an emphasis on prevention (Cordner 2014; TRILLION: TRusted, CItizen – LEA coILaboratIon over social Networks 2017). Naturally, this approach puts pressure at organizational level, for moving from a top-down approach of police management to a bottom-up approach, where citizens have a more active role. Another challenge relates to trust within and between the law enforcement agencies and the citizens. Motivation for engaging citizens in this community driven policing framework is also crucial. Community policing has been used successfully in crime reduction (Gill et al. 2014), extremism prevention (Schanzer et al. 2016), and even in counter terrorism (Dunn et al. 2016). In all cases, it was based on direct face-to-face or over-the-phone interaction between the community and LEAs. There is a growing realization that technology has the potential to accelerate the evolution towards more effective community policing (Lewis and Lewis 2012).

TRILLION takes the concept of technology-assisted community policing further and is currently developing a community policing platform, which aims to contribute to a safer society, encouraging interactive partnerships between law enforcement officers and the people they serve, implemented over an open, flexible, secure and resilient socio-technical set of tools. Using the TRILLION applications, citizens will be able to report crimes, suspicious behavior and incidents, identify hazards and assist law enforcement agents through active participation for achieving better urban security management. At the same time, LEAs will be able to detect incidents in a more efficient, content and context aware manner, and locate onsite

Fig. 1.1 Use of technology
and societal approval (RAND
quadrants)

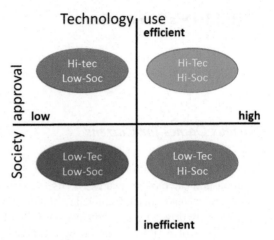

citizens. Community policing technology can improve effectiveness and efficiency
but, if used incorrectly, could be perceived as intrusive, losing public support. For a
starting point on how LEAs and Citizens collaborate towards a safer society, and to
focus on a plausible future, the approach proposed by the RAND Corporation[1] has
been adopted. RAND used several techniques to develop their scenarios, presented
in a matrix where each axis represents extremes at one side, enabling each quadrant
to represent a clear and distinct scenario domain.

To establish a reliable scenario framework and having in mind the importance
of trust between citizens and LEAs, the adoption of the methodology proposed by
RAND (Siberglitt et al. 2015) represents a key factor. RAND's chart is based on the
observation that the most important factors driving the future of law enforcement fall
into two categories: Technology and Society. The effectiveness of the technology
used by LEAs to accomplice their missions depends on the level of technology
(vertical axis) and the extent to which LEA practices are accepted by society
(horizontal axis). As presented in Fig. 1.1, the quadrants delimited by technology
and society, create four different situations/futures, where moving to the upper
right corner is the target for the serious games. In the Hi-Tec/Hi-Soc (upper right)
quadrant, LEAs use advanced technology for dealing with different situations, enjoy
societal support by the public. In the Low-Tec/Hi-Soc (lower right) quadrant, LEAs
use obsolete technologies, but society continues to support them. In the Hi-Tec/Low-
Soc (upper left) quadrant, LEAs have the advantage in use of technology, but have
lost society's trust, which opposes every action they take. In the Low-Tec/Low-Soc
(lower left) quadrant, LEAs use old technologies, and have to face a society which
opposes every LEA measure and action.

[1]Silberglitt R, Brian G. Chow, John S. Hollywood, Dulani Woods, Mikhail Zaydman and Brian
A. Jackson. Visions of Law Enforcement Technology in the Period 2024-2034: Report of the Law
Enforcement Futuring Workshop. Santa Monica, CA: RAND Corporation,: 2015.

TRILLION's Serious Games

The TRILLION serious games were designed to be simple, easy to use, and enabling and facilitating best practices proposed in community policing.

Serious Games for Citizens

The serious game platform/application for citizens focuses on location, communication and interaction awareness. Its scenarios were designed having in mind technological and societal challenges taking into account the RAND approach. Scenarios are driven by how advances in technology are adopted and by how laws and LEAs evolve and are viewed by the public, which determines the effects of the evolution of society on law enforcement. At the end of the game, citizens are encouraged to download the mobile and wearable TRILLION apps and use them in real life to be engaged in community policing.

Game Scenarios The implemented scenarios are represented by non-linear storytelling, and supported by location-based mobile technologies, that will allow players to interact with virtual characters and items across an area. Virtual items collected during the gaming session will be used by players when they face the virtual event. Through creative entertainment, the serious games creators/masters, convey a positive message and "recommended behaviours" in the specific circumstances implemented in a scenario, which should be meaningful and realistic.

Architecture The architectural solution implemented for serious games is the client-server model. The client runs on mobile personal devices for the computational part, while the server side provides data regarding the games' list and data model linked to a game (items, characters, events, requirements, actions).

Game Elements The main game elements are *items*, which are objects scattered within the boundaries of the game area and are not always useful towards the game's goal (they could be used by the game master to divert the player's attention); *characters*, which are virtual people usually linked with an audio file; *events*, which need the citizen's reaction; and *actions*, which are selected by the player once an event position is reached. At the end of the game, a debriefing session allows to learn different/better behaviors and evaluates whether the goals were achieved, including fostering collaborative gameplay and behavior; and increase citizen awareness on collaboration with LEAs.

Communities For enabling the engagement and the collaboration of citizens/players, a community service has been created. The purpose is to stimulate discussions around the themes of the project and to enhance and strengthen the LEOs – Citizens relationship, especially for convincing reluctant citizens who see LEO's authority as an intrusion in their lives.

Serious Games for LEAs

The purpose of the game was to develop the skills of the LEOs in interacting with the public using the TRILLION solutions, and because its focus is on community partnership and the future use of technology by both citizens and the police, the game could be considered to sit in the Hi-Tec/Hi-Soc, upper right corner of the RAND quadrant. The scenario chosen was on antisocial behavior, which was was felt to be important to all participating end users, in contrast to what would be a more rare event, such as a terrorist incident. To ensure the design of the game scenario was as realistic as possible, an Senior Policing, Border and Security Consultant was engaged to design the game scenario. The game platform used was Pandora$^+$ (Bacon et al. 2017), originally developed for the 2010–2012 EU FP7 project entitled "Advanced Training Environment for Crisis Scenarios" (Bacon et al. 2012a, b; Mackinnon et al. 2013). The Pandora$^+$ training tool is a cloud-based client-server system which runs on a desktop or mobile device. Whilst it can be used in multiple ways, there are two core modes of use: (a) With a trainer of a group of people all working through the same game scenario, or (b) with trainees working through their own game scenario independently of a trainer. For this game, the second mode was deemed the most appropriate, i.e. each LEA trainee would play their own game. The Pandora$^+$ training tool is designed to provide an immersive multimedia experience to the player(s), and works by delivering an unfolding series of events as a situation develops, that requires LEA involvement. An example is a TRILLION citizen reporting on a fight breaking out who submits details of the suspect to the police through the TRILLION platform, sending in pictures of the incident or describing a suspect etc. The role of the trainee is to decide the appropriate TRILLION-relevant communication with the citizens, to reassure them, warn them or get further information. Note that the Pandora$^+$ tool has the capability to change the scenario and outcomes depending on how the player responds at different points in the game, if appropriate.

Learning Outcomes The focus of the game for the LEOs was on the communication with the citizen and their ability to compose appropriate messages when presented with different situations and responses from citizens. The learning outcomes identified for this training exercise were designed to enable the trainee to:

1. Utilise TRILLION in line with its core objectives.
2. Appreciate how a social media TRILLION-style police communication tool can assist community policing objectives and outcomes.
3. Create balanced and appropriate public safety communication messages.
4. Create balanced and appropriate messages for mobilising support from citizens for community safety goals and police efficiency.
5. Create balanced and appropriate messages for mobilising support from citizens for police investigation goals & police efficiency.

Game Elements

Characters The LEO (being trained), four citizens who witness the anti-social behaviour, community police colleagues, paramedics, trusted TRILLION users and two security professionals.

Events These represent something that is happening, which may just be information or a situation update, or may require a response or action by the trainee.

Action During the scenario, the trainees were asked for six text responses which they had to compose, regarding their use of the TRILLION services.

Execution of the Game The final version of the scenario was entitled "Episode in the day of a community police officer" and lasted for about 13 min. The length was designed to be manageable within an appropriate timeframe / attention span of the participants, without making it too complex, whilst also being sufficient to achieve the learning outcomes. The games were designed separately to ensure a consistent experience for both the citizens and the LEOs thus allowing the performance of each participant to be appropriately evaluated within the group, as everyone would have the same experience.

The game was run in Lisbon, York, Ancona, Lecce and Eindhoven, and the scenario was presented to the participants in their native language. Participants were also able to respond in their native language and the results were translated into English so they could be analysed by the same team to ensure consistency. Tablets were used by the LEOs to access the system. There was also one person who was present at all the trials to ensure they were conducted in a consistent manner. In terms of the actual game playing event, a briefing was provided to the LEOs beforehand on what they would experience and how to access the system. Once the game was started by the LEO, the events were delivered at fixed times (the participants were unable to slow down or speed up). After the game was finished, the person running the training session ran a debriefing session which was an important part of the learning. The scenario author had provided guidance on the key aspects to look for in the messages sent by the LEOs, such as whether it was clear who the message was sent from and directed to, whether the LEO made the type of incident, the location and timing clear, whether the request of an intended recipient was appropriately concise, clear and unambiguous, whether the LEO sought to reassure a citizen to mitigate a sense of undue fear, whether the Police message / request was balanced and proportionate to the type of incident / action requested and relevant to required policing goals, etc. The scenario also provided an example of a good answer for each of the six messages required of the LEOs. A discussion about how each person had approached this, what they thought was important in each message etc. was discussed.

Results

Since the scope of the games is to move the citizens' position to the upper right corner in the quadrant, the same questionnaire was submitted twice: before and after playing. The questionnaire included questions to investigate social aspects and position Citizens' perception in the RAND quadrant. The number of LEOs at each event ranged from 9 to 15 and the number of citizens from 20 to 25. When the responses were analysed, the match was not high and not all responses were complete. There were a number of explanations for this, firstly the time to respond was relatively short, there are cultural differences in the style of police communication and police officers are generally not trained in this style of communication with the public. In some cases, the LEOs did not come as a group but in couples during the day, which might have affected their approach and attitude. Overall, the LEOs were positive about the TRILLION functionalities and their use in everyday life. According to citizens' and LEOs' answers to the questionnaire, due to reported constraints, the real initial position of the test bed communities was set in the middle with a slight propensity to the right hand side (Fig. 1.2). In summary, the public is often concerned with immediate response to incidents, there is a lack of explanation as to when and why technology is used, and there is little sharing of information. Also, response times can be slow.

After playing, the same questionnaire was submitted to the players for the second time. The responses were analysed and the new position, as expected, was in the upper right hand quadrant.

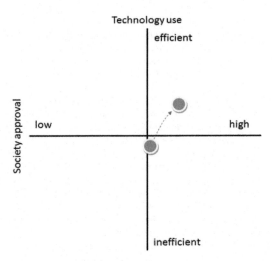

Fig. 1.2 Initial and final position (before and after playing)

Conclusions

Community policing is gradually becoming synonymous to modern policing, but from a technological perspective, this process is supported by disjointed local initiatives, including collaborative software tools and social media monitoring services coming from National and European research initiatives like TRILLION. In particular TRILLION, serious games are used to train and educate the community in order to stimulate discussion and create awareness around the community policing mechanisms and plans and to transform the LEA-Citizen relationship for the better, especially welcoming and encouraging citizens who see LEO's authority as an intrusion in their lives. Serious games constitute an ambitious offering, whose components are already evaluated in live trials in several locations in Europe, and in close collaboration with a variety of LEAs. The RAND document was used to understand the effectiveness of serious games. While the results coming from the serious games for citizens helped us to detect the initial and the final position of the citizens in the RAND chart, the results coming from the serious games for LEAs could be appreciated only after a long-term period.

Acknowledgments This work is funded by the European Commission under grant number H2020-FCT-2014, REA grant agreement n° [653256]. The support is gratefully acknowledged.

References

Bacon, L., MacKinnon, L., Cesta, A., & Cortellessa, G. (2012a). Developing a smart environment for crisis management training. Special edition of the *Journal of Ambient Intelligence and Humanized Computing*, entitled Smart Environments and Collective Computational Intelligence for Disaster Management, *3*(2). https://doi.org/10.1007/s12652-012-0124-0.

Bacon, L., Cesta, A., Coraci, L., Cortellessa, G., Benedictis, R. D., Grilli, S., Polutnik, J., & Strickland, K. (2012b, August). Training crisis managers with PANDORA. In *ECAI, the Biennial European Conference on Artificial Intelligence* (pp. 27–31). Montpelier, France.

Bacon, L., MacKinnon, L., & Kananda, D. Supporting real-time decision making under stress in an online training environment. Published Feb 2017 in *The IEEE Journal of Latin-American Learning Technologies (IEEE-RITA, IEEE – Revista Iberoamericana de Tecnologias del Aprendizaje)* (Vol. 12, No. 1, pp. 52–61). Print ISSN: 1932–8540. Online ISSN: 1932–8540. Digital Object Identifier: https://doi.org/10.1109/RITA.2017.2659021.

COPS – U.S. Department of Justice. (2014). *Community policing defined* [Online]. Available at: ric-zai-inc.com/Publications/cops-p157-pub.pdf.

Cordner, G. (2014). Community policing. In M. D. Reisig & R. J. Kane (Eds.), *The Oxford handbook of police and policing* (pp. 148–171). Oxford: Oxford University Press.

Crime Stoppers International. https://csiworld.org/. Last accessed on August 2017.

Dunn, K. M., Atie, R., Kennedy, M., Ali, J. A., O'Reilly, J., & Rogerson, L. (2016). Can you use community policing for counter terrorism? Evidence from NSW, Australia. *Police Practice and Research, 17*(3), 196–211.

Gill, C., Weisburd, D., Telep, C. W., Vitter, Z., & Bennett, T. (2014). Community-oriented policing to reduce crime, disorder and fear and increase satisfaction and legitimacy among citizens: A systematic review. *Journal of Experimental Criminology, 10*(4), 399.

Lewis, S., & Lewis, D. A. (2012, May). Examining technology that supports community policing. In *Proceedings of the SIGCHI Conference on Human Factors in Computing Systems* (pp. 1371–1380). ACM.

Mackinnon, L., Bacon, L., Cortellessa, G., Cesta, A. (2013, May). Using emotional intelligence in training crisis managers: The Pandora approach. *The International Journal of Distance Education Technologies (IJDET)*, *11*(2), 66–95, IGI Global.

Patrikakis, C., Konstantas, A., Kogias, D., & Choras, M. (2017). *TRILLION project approach on scenarios definition for citizen security services*. To appear in International Journal of Electronic Governance.

Schanzer, D. H., Kurzman, C., Toliver, J., & Miller, E. (2016). *The challenge and promise of using community policing strategies to prevent violent extremism: A call for community partnerships with law enforcement to enhance public safety*. Durham: Triangle Center on Terrorism and Homeland Security.

Siberglitt, R., Chow, B. G., Hollywood, J. S., Woods, D., Zaydman, M., & Jackson, B. A. (2015). *Visions of law enforcement technology in the period 2024–2034*. Santa Monica: RAND Corporation.

TRILLION: TRusted, CItizen – LEA coILaboratIon over social Networks. (2017). http://trillion-project.eng.it. Deliverable 2.1 "Creation and Management of User Community"

Chapter 2
Can Technology Build Trust? Community-Oriented Policing and ICT in Afghanistan

Ajmal Nimruzi, Jaishankar Ganapathy, and Ingrid L. P. Nyborg

Introduction: The Scene

One of the most pressing problems in post-conflict societies is the establishment of trust between the police and citizens. Trust levels are low, and in many cases police services themselves are perpetuators of abuse and violence against communities. Afghanistan is also a case in point. To tackle this problem both Ministry of Interior Afghanistan (MoIA) and the police have taken several measures to facilitate better cooperation between police services and communities. At the heart of these measures is the establishment of community-oriented policing (COP). As a policing model its relevance lies in building trust and legitimacy in police/ community relations. The use of information and communication technology (ICT) is an important step in this direction.

A. Nimruzi (✉)
ICT4COP Project led, Norwegian University of Life Sciences, Ås, Norway
e-mail: ajmal.nimruzi@nca.no

J. Ganapathy
Norwegian Police University College, Oslo, Norway
e-mail: jaigan@phs.no

I. L. P. Nyborg
Department of International Environment and Development Studies, Norwegian University of Life Sciences, Ås, Norway
e-mail: ingrid.nyborg@nmbu.no

© The Author(s) 2018   11
G. Leventakis, M. R. Haberfeld (eds.), *Community-Oriented Policing and Technological Innovations*, SpringerBriefs in Criminology,
https://doi.org/10.1007/978-3-319-89294-8_2

Scope of the Paper

This paper will explore the motivation, workings and potential effect of the police's use of various information and communication technologies to build trust in Afghanistan. Do these efforts in fact contribute to trust-building and broader human security? What happens to trust-building when it comes to technology mediated interaction? In addition to the police, we look at ICT solutions being developed by civil society that also aim at improving better relations between police and government.

Research Methodology and Approach

Data collection for this paper involves in-depth interviews, focus group discussions and participant observations of meetings and conferences. The data was collected between November 2015 and April 2017 covering Kabul and the province of Nimruz. In both places we conducted interviews with representatives from MoIA, international stakeholders, civil society organizations (CSOs) and non-governmental organizations (NGOs). In addition we also refer to secondary data from research papers, reports and policy documents.

ICT and Policing

One of the main uses of technology by the police is to enhance their effectiveness in solving crimes. This is also an important objective within post-conflict police reform. Different eras in policing have witnessed technological advancements in combating crimes. For example, in the 30s introduction of two way radio communications, 90s the use of fingerprinting and within criminal investigation storage, retrieval, transfer and application of investigation related information (Fox 2016; Hekim et al. 2013). Recently, the use of mobile applications to report crime is also being explored. Different periods have witnessed different technological contributions and advancements within policing to help solve crimes.

Social media in particular, although new in its form, is gaining momentum and becoming quite prevalent in policing. Bartlett et al. (2013) identify three avenues on the use of social media by the police: intelligence, enforcement and engagement. In our paper the focus is on the use of ICTs for engagement and trust-building between police and communities. The use of social media by the police offers new possibilities of engagement with communities by way of contact, information sharing and instant participation on issues of safety and security. This is not an easy task in post-conflict contexts where citizen's perception and trust-levels of police are low. Our aim is to critically view how police and civil society in a post-conflict society such as Afghanistan can mutually benefit from ICTs in ensuring human security.

Human Security and Trust

Although the focus of using ICT is often on crime identification, reporting and prevention, enhancing police relations is equally important. Myhill reminds us of the importance of community engagement:

> The process of enabling the participation of citizens and communities in policing at their chosen level, ranging from providing information and reassurance, to empowering them to identify and implement solutions to local problems and influence strategic priorities and decisions. The police, citizens, and communities must have the willingness, capacity and opportunity to participate. (Myhill 2006, p. 01)

Research has pointed out how trust building and legitimacy are both crucial for community-police relations to be effective and fruitful (Sherman 1997; Stoutland 2001; Tyler and Huo 2002). Several studies have shown that citizen cooperation is vital for good and effective policing (Cordner 1997; Greene and Pelfry 1997; Skogan 1998). COP is an important policing model that can facilitate better cooperation and trust between the police and community (Alderson 1977, 1979; Bennett 1994; Greene 2000). In addition, citizen's perceptions of the police are greatly enhanced by their contact with the police (Cheurprakobkit 2000; Hawdon and Ryan 2003). The crucial question is how ICT can facilitate the above mentioned outcomes in post-conflict countries where trust and legitimacy are low.

A human security approach captures the various challenges of insecurities experienced by different people. Central to the understanding is the focus on the security of populations rather than the security of the state. The concept facilitates the understanding of police-community relations involving different actors and institutions at all levels. It is in this context one has to view the role of ICTs in reducing human insecurities and strengthening the relations between police and communities. Although there are a number of advantages in the use of ICTs, there are also risks involved in such emerging technologies especially in fragile societies trying to cope with trust, security and reconstruction challenges. Some of the risks are; the use of ICTs by an unaccountable police causing more insecurity, lack of a guarantee of safety for those using such technologies and the lack of protection of data generated through ICTs in terms of who has access to it. Without community engagement and support, the use of ICTs in building a safe environment would be fruitless.

Afghan Security Sector and ICT

MoIA in 2013 envisioned a ten-year plan to reform the Afghan National Police (ANP) from a 'militarized' unit for combating terrorism and counter-insurgency to a 'service' unit. Community-Oriented Policing (COP) was at the heart of this vision. The use of technology on the part of MoIA is a step in this direction.

The use of traditional media bettering the image between the police and citizens has been in use for some time. For example, an NGO interviewed in Kabul explained how they invited a police representative to their radio show to facilitate direct interaction between the police and communities. Also, a radio channel called 'Radio Police' was launched by MoIA with the intent of bettering communication and contact between the police and public (Zaland 2015). In addition, MoIA[1] has been developing their Media and Outreach Directorate to perform better outreach to citizens and improve transparency.

In 2009, MoIA launched the helpline 119 as their first major ICT initiative. The line was originally designed with the aim of assisting citizens to help them make complaints against police misbehavior, corruption and human rights violations. It later included the reporting of criminal and terrorist activities. In 2013 the line was extended to five other provinces. In order to create public awareness about the existence of the line, a private TV channel had a TV program called 'Show Reaction 119' (Zaland 2015). Still, however, there are no 119 units in most of the provinces.

Despite increasing awareness and use of the helpline, both ethical and technical shortcomings have been pointed out by MoIA officials and NGO representatives. Some of the technical shortcomings identified were lack of sufficient maintenance and support systems. People manning the call centers are not professional police, causing delays in action to be taken. On the ethical side the biggest challenge is, as mentioned by NGO leaders, safeguarding the identity of the caller and controlling who has access to all the incoming data.

In 2013, MoIA launched a Facebook and Twitter page. These are forums where the police can inform of their activities and people can comment on them, and people can also inform the police about security issues or problems occurring in the neighborhood and even post films showing the police catching criminals.

From our field studies in Nimruz Province, examples from the Shuras[2] in the city show how communities in partnership with the police help to curb crimes and insurgencies. An important step in this preventive measure is the provision of cell phone numbers of the police to Shura members who can now call upon them anytime in case of an emergency.

These efforts on the part of the Government may look small and insignificant. However, keeping the context of Afghanistan as a conflict/post-conflict society facing insurmountable challenges on the issues of trust, security, corruption and accountability in mind, such measures can nevertheless contribute to improving relations between police and communities. What is important to note, however, is that these technologies are only useful if they are initiated in a context of mutual trust – they need a trusted relationship to begin with, and then may build trust over

[1] With the assistance of a private consulting firm through the Strategic Support Ministry of Interior (SSMI) project.

[2] A local committee of respected community members.

time if communication continues. The question to be asked then is how to build enough trust between communities and the police such that ICTs will in fact enhance this trust.

Civil Society, the Police and ICTs

It should be mentioned that civil society was involved with Afghanistan National Security Forces (ANSF) and other government agencies in various projects following the Bonn agreement in 2001, but these efforts were scattered and there was no institutionalized relationship between the two.

This changed with the implementation of the Democratic Policing or Community Policing Pilot[3] in 2009. To design this project, civil society organizations conducted consultations with diverse stakeholders including parliamentarians, NGOs, civil society organizations, media, academics and different community members representing vulnerable groups like women, children and ethnic minorities. The program was called Police e Mardumi (PEM) (ISSAT–DCAF 2017). Later this program turned into a permanent Community Policing Directorate at the Afghanistan Ministry of Interior. Civil society along with Afghan media in collaboration with MoIA launched awareness campaigns by using mobile phones, social media, TV and radio plays to highlight the importance of citizen initiatives regarding issues of safety and security (ISSAT-DCAF 2017).

While civil society organizations were instrumental in eventual creation of the Community Policing Unit in MOIA, their further involvement with Community Policing came with the implementation of the Afghanistan Democratic Policing Project (ADPP). This three-year project was initiated in 2013 and involved several national and international NGOs, coordinated through UNAMA[4], UNOPS[5] and UNDP[6]. The activities in this bold and engaging project were diverse and covered many different aspects of community-police relations.[7]

ICT tools become important when it comes to issues like gender barriers. This was highlighted by a leading Afghan female ICT entrepreneur interviewed in Kabul. In 2010 she set up a software company as a non-profit organization in Herat Province of Afghanistan to teach girls and women about computers, programming, financial literacy and business skills. Although such initiatives may not be directly related to

---

[3]Use of Democratic Policing instead of Community policing was to avoid confusion between Local Police and Community Policing- Local Police is rather a "Militia" Force envisioned to defend population centers at the local level.

[4]United Nations Assistance Mission in Afghanistan.

[5]United Nations Office for Project Services.

[6]United Nations Development Programme.

[7]From series of document received from United Nations Office for Project Services (UNOPS) Afghanistan office.

policing, such efforts open avenues of cooperation and trust-building between civil society and government organizations. In a conservative society like Afghanistan where women may not be allowed to move outside their houses, access to ICT tools like radio, mobile phones and internet could be considered a positive sign.

Police Engagement with Civil Society ICT Efforts

Afghan civil society has been successfully able to mobilize public engagement and support on a variety of issues. For example, Integrity Watch Afghanistan launched a website in 2015 where common people could visit and register their complaints regarding government conduct. The website acted as a whistle-blower. Complaints could be registered through email, SMS, Call, Website and Facebook page.

Collaboration between the police and civil society is challenging, and direct links between the police and civil society may be too risky when trust remains an issue. In such cases, combining information collected by civil society along with face-to-face interactions between civil society and the police can be an appropriate model to build awareness, trust and legitimacy. More challenging is the relationship at the national level, where security actors have a strong position in determining government policy. Recently, through the efforts from the international community, there have nevertheless been some major achievements in developing good and stable relationships between civil society and ANSF (army, police, and intelligence). In 2016 for example, MoIA and Afghanistan Human Rights Commission (AHRC) signed a MoU that facilitates AHRC to conduct observation into the conduct of the Security and Defence Organizations.

Conclusions

Addressing issues of security and insecurity within post-conflict contexts is not easy. A well-functioning police service as providers of security, safety and justice to all citizens is an important institution for successful state building. An important step towards community engagement between authorities and police has been the use of ICTs. Central to these efforts has been the various initiatives taken by MoIA. We also pointed out different challenges involved in using ICTs in post-conflict contexts. However, for technologies to be effective there needs to be a certain level of trust between the police and the communities. The role of civil society in this process is central since they have knowledge and experience of people's insecurities and distrust. The collaboration between civil society and police in using ICTs is challenging, but our research shows that it can be feasible and contribute to community engagement, better communication and mutual trust building.

References

Alderson, J. (1977). *Communal policing*. Exeter: Devon and Cornwall Constabulary.

Alderson, J. (1979). *Policing freedom*. Plymouth: Macdonald & Evans.

Bartlett, J., Miller, C., Crump, J., & Middleton, L. (2013). *Policing in the information age*. London: Demos.

Bennett, T. (1994). Community policing on the ground: Developments in Britain. In D. Rosenbaum (Ed.), *The challenge of community policing* (pp. 224–246). Thousand Oakes: Sage.

Cheurprakobkit, S. (2000). Police-citizen contact and police performance: Attitudinal differences between Hispanics and non-Hispanics. *Journal of Criminal Justice, 28*, 325–336.

Cordner, G. (1997). Community policing: Elements and effects. In R. Durham & G. Alpert (Eds.), *Critical issues in policing: Contemporary readings* (3rd ed., pp. 451–468). Prospect Heughts: Waveland.

Fox, C. (2016). *How do the police use ICT to solve crimes?* Retrieved from https://prezi.com/i6yejcteitb5/how-do-the-police-use-ict-to-solve-crimes/

Government of Islamic Republic of Afghanistan, Ministry of Interior Affairs. *Ten-year vision for the Afghan National Police: 1392–1402*. Retrieved from http://moi.gov.af/en/page/5718/5729

Government of Islamic Republic of Afghanistan, Ministry of Interior Affairs, Deputy Ministry for Strategy and Policy, General Directorate of Strategy. (2015). *Ministry of Interior Strategy for the years 1394–1398 (2015–2019), February 2015.* Retrieved from https://globalnetplatform.org/system/files/50121/MIS%20-%20English%2001%20March%202015%20%28Strategy%20-%20Policy%29_2.pdf

Greene, J. (2000). Community policing in America: Changing the nature, structure, and function of the police. In J. Horney (Ed.), *Policies, processes and decisions of the criminal justice system*, Criminal Justice 2000 (pp. 299–370). Washington, DC: US Department of Justice Office of Justice Programs.

Greene, J., & Pelfry, W. V. (1997). Shifting the balance of power between police and community: Responsibility for crime control. In R. Dunham & G. Alpert (Eds.), *Critical issues in policing: Contemporary readings* (3rd ed., pp. 393–423). Prospect Heights: Waveland.

Hawdon, J., & Ryan, J. (2003). Police-resident interactions and satisfactions with police: An empirical test of community policing assertions. *Criminal Justice Policy Review, 14*, 55–74.

Hekim, H., Gul, S. K., & Akcam, B. K. (2013). Police use of information technologies in criminal investigations. *European Scientific Journal February edition, 9*(4), 221–240.

ISSAT-DECAF. (2017). *Afghanistan: 'Democratic policing'*. Retrieved from http://issat.dcaf.ch/Learn/Resource-Library/Case-Studies/Afghanistan-Democratic-Policing

Myhill, A. (2006). *Community engagement in policing: Lessons from the literature*. London: Home Office.

Sherman, L. W. (1997). Communities and crime prevention. In L. Sherman, D. Gottfredson, D. MacKenzie, J. Eck, P. Reuter, & S. Bushway (Eds.), *Preventing crime: What works, what doesn't, what's promising* (pp. 58–109). Washington, DC: Department of Justice.

Skogan, W. G. (1998). Community participation and community policing. In J. P. Brodeur (Ed.), *How to recognize good policing: Problems and issues* (pp. 88–106). Thousand Oaks: Sage.

Stoutland, S. E. (2001). The multiple dimensions of trust in resident-police relations in Boston. *Journal of Research in Crime and Delinquency, 38*, 513–547.

Tyler, T. R., & Huo, Y. J. (2002). *Trust in the law: Encouraging public cooperation with the police and courts*. New York: Russell Sage.

Zaland, S. (2015). *Building trust between police and public through community out-reach program*. Retrieved from: http://www.afghanjustice.org/article/articledetail/building-trust-between-police-and-public-through-community-outreach-programs

Chapter 3
Community Outreach Using Incident Records and Visual Analytics

Chittayong Surakitbanharn, José F. de Queiroz Neto, Guizhen Wang, and David S. Ebert

Introduction

Poor perception of law enforcement can strain the overall relationship between law enforcement and the community; however, transparency of law enforcement actions can solve these problems and the availability of police data provides new opportunities (Forst 2008; Scheider et al. 2003). Unfortunately, police record databases are often cumbersome to navigate and do not have built-in interactive capabilities. As a result, there lacks a readily available way for law enforcement to explore CAD and RMS data for policing strategy evaluation and community outreach. To address this challenge, we have designed, deployed, and tested the Visual Analytics Law Enforcement Toolkit (VALET) to aid officers in data exploration.

Initially, VALET was designed for internal use within a police department to understand crime trends and aid in resource allocation decision-making. However, Crime Prevention Specialists, who primarily interface with the community, are utilizing VALET as a visual tool in community meetings to address public questions about crime incident trends and statistics. Below, we overview recent community policing techniques, VALET and its features, and report the outcomes and challenges of our efforts to use visual analytic crime data software to shape public perception.

C. Surakitbanharn · G. Wang · D. S. Ebert (✉)
VACCINE – Visual Analytics for Command, Control and Interoperability Environments, Potter Engineering Center, Purdue University, West Lafayette, IN, USA
e-mail: csurakit@purdue.edu; wang1908@purdue.edu; ebertd@ecn.purdue.edu

J. F. de Queiroz Neto
CRAb – Computer Graphics, Virtual Reality and Animation, Computer Science Department, Federal University of Ceará, Fortaleza, Brazil
e-mail: florencio@lia.ufc.br

© The Author(s) 2018   19
G. Leventakis, M. R. Haberfeld (eds.), *Community-Oriented Policing and Technological Innovations*, SpringerBriefs in Criminology,
https://doi.org/10.1007/978-3-319-89294-8_3

Perceptions of Community Policing

The standard approach to fighting crime was traditionally based on a large number of police officers, random patrols, and reaction to incidents (Weisburd and Eck 2004). However, these methods are being replaced by more broad sighted and focused strategies, such as Community Policing, Problem Oriented Policing, and Hot Spot Policing. Community policing is a strategy that believes community members and the police, working together, can better resolve problems related to crime as well as physical and social disorder (Trojanowicz and Bucqueroux 1990). However, community policing is not without controversy, as critics cite a lack of causal evidence between community policing and crime reduction (Coquilhat 2008). Furthermore, despite engagement efforts, residents may still not perceive police as effective or active in policing their neighborhood or another region. Our law enforcement partners in Lafayette, IN cited comments during community meetings about "feeling" the rise of crime in a particular area, despite contrary records data. Without real-time analytical tools, officers are unable to empirically support or test such claims about crime trends. The lack of data creates a back-and-forth interaction with the community where both officers and the public believe the other side is making unsubstantiated claims, which can strain the relationship between officers and the public.

Problem Oriented Policing

Problem Oriented Policing (POP) expands police activities and relationships to include communities and other government agencies, collaboratively working to understand and address the underlying conditions of recurring crimes (Braga 2014). In this context, a problem is a social or systemic condition that continuously generates clusters of criminal incidents.

The POP approach first identifies an overarching problem, such as an opioid epidemic that leads to drug arrests, and then examines all factors that might contribute to the problem. In the opioid example, unintended addiction resulting from prescription drugs may lead to opioid related incidents. Together with the community and other agencies, the POP approach defines, implements, and continuously evaluates possible solutions, such as the increased regulation of prescription drugs. A challenge with POP is evaluating the impact of solutions, with few rigorous evaluations available (Weisburd et al. 2010). Data exploration tools can help evaluate and convey the impact of the POP approach on crime incidents, especially for multiple criteria.

Hot Spot Policing

Hot spot policing allocates more officers and resources to areas with higher crime rates. It is based on the idea that certain areas have a higher concentration of incidents and tend to remain consistent over time (Weisburd et al. 2012). Knowledge of these areas can both simplify patrol decision making and contribute to crime reduction (Weisburd and Eck 2004), with minimal displacement of criminal activity to neighboring regions (Braga 2001).

Nevertheless, concentrating officers at hot spots can lead to law-abiding citizens in the vicinity feeling unfairly targeted. Without empirical data and community outreach, the rationale for an increased police presence may be unclear to the community and even misconstrued as racial profiling. Such feelings may reduce goodwill and trust towards the police officers, and create obstacles in community policing. In a similar vein to the community policing problem, there has been a lack of interactive technology to show hot spots and address community questions in real time.

Crime Mapping Technologies

CrimeStat IV, GeoDa, ESRI Public Safety Incident Maps, and Crime Reports are currently available analytical tools that are limited in their broader use. For example, CrimeStat IV provides hundreds of statistical analysis modules to capture trends (Levine 2013), but lacks a built-in visualization component. As such, the tool does not lend itself to real-time analyses by a larger section of the police department.

GeoDa is a free tool designed for general spatial analyses and it is not specialized for law enforcement data and lacks features designed for exploratory data analysis of crime incidents (Leitner and Brecht 2007). It can, however, display visual analyses as a freestanding software, making it more accessible to the public.

ESRI offers tools on their commercial GIS platform dedicated to law enforcement activities including, Public Safety Incident Maps, Repeat and Near Repeat Analysis, and Manage Community Events. These tools are designed for specialized use rather real-time crime data analysis.

In contrast, CrimeReports is a web-based collection and spatial visualization of crime datasets in the United States. Public users can filter incidents by date, time, and event type in CrimeReports, but limitations hinder more in-depth analysis. First, the public interface only displays the last six months of data, making it impossible to compare trends over several years. Second, incidents are displayed at the block level rather than at the actual location, creating ambiguity about the location of occurrences. Third, CrimeReports does not allow the creation of boundaries around a neighborhood to capture a total amount of crimes for a certain area or the differences in crimes for that area at different periods of time.

Individual tools may have strengths in analytical capabilities or usability, but prior technologies are not designed to find a balance between the two traits. Moreover, the tools can be difficult for an officer to use in a community meeting to address questions in real time. As a response to these shortcomings, our law enforcement partners and our team brought VALET to community meetings for initial testing of whether it would improve public perception of law enforcement actions.

Community Outreach with VALET

Officers can encounter challenges in shaping community perception with a lack of empirical evidence to support claims of improved performance or a reduction in crime. Partnering with the Lafayette Police Department (Indiana, USA), we attempted to bridge the perception gap between the community and the police department through real-time use of the VALET.

VALET was originally designed and tested for internal use by a police department to facilitate interactive and visual spatiotemporal exploration of crime, traffic, and civil incident reports (Malik 2014; Wang et al. 2017).

At the center of the VALET display (Fig. 3.1, view e) is a map view that aggregates and displays the spatial crime distribution. Additionally, VALET displays the

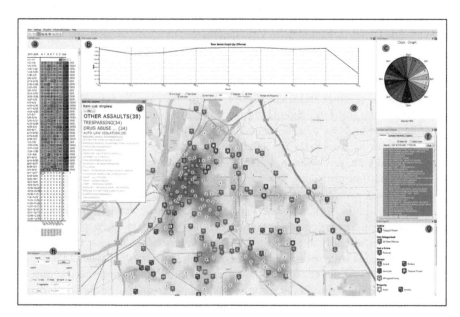

Fig. 3.1 VALET's main interface is composed of interactive interconnected views: in (**a**) calendar view, in (**b**) time series line view, in (**c**) clock view, in (**d**) rank view, in (**e**) main map and incidents view, in (**f**) incident type selection view, in (**g**) icon dictionary view and in (**h**) we have the time slider view

total number of crimes by day of the week for every week of the year (Fig. 3.1, view a), incident trends over time (Fig. 3.1, view b), and a clock view (Fig. 3.1, view c) that shows hourly crime distribution. VALET can display selections of data for a certain period, geography, crime, or a combination of these factors. The function at the center left filters the data by time (Fig. 3.1, view h), drawing a boundary on the displayed map selects a region, and the right window (Fig. 3.1, view f) facilitates crime selection.

Real Time Data Analysis

In June 2017, VALET's developers accompanied the Lafayette Police Department (LPD) to three community meetings to use the VALET to answer community questions.

To conduct the crime comparison with VALET, the operator first drew a boundary around a neighborhood and surrounding areas, and selected three different periods: the first half of 2016, the second half of 2016, and the first half of 2017. VALET extracted a copy of the crime incidents from the RMS database and returned the query to the audience in real time, as shown in Fig. 3.2.

Figure 3.2 indicates rising crime trends for the selected region, as seen in the total at the top of the map view. In the selected boundary, the first half of 2016 reported a total of 270 crimes, the second half of 2016 reported a total of 293 crimes, and the first half of 2017 reported a total of 306 crimes. The map and clock views showed insignificant spatiotemporal changes in overall incidents.

The rank view indicated that 'Auto Law Violation' was the most prevalent incident in the first half of 2016 with 23 incidents, but decreased to ten incidents in the second half of 2016, and 18 incidents in the first half of 2017. Additionally, 'Other Assaults' increased by 25% to be the leading crime incident in the first half of 2017. A closer evaluation of the 'Other Assault' trends between the second half of 2016 and the first half of 2017 indicated that incidents became more concentrated at one particular apartment complex. The increase in incidents is visually displayed

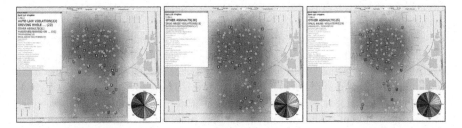

Fig. 3.2 VALET example: The image represents all crime incidents for a neighborhood in Lafayette, Indiana, the USA for the first half of 2016 (left), second half of 2016 (middle), and first half of 2017 (right). Each map has three views: rank view, map view and clock view

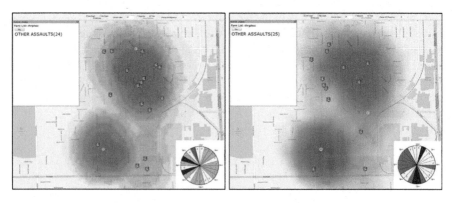

Fig. 3.3 VALET example: 'Other Assaults' incidents at two different date ranges for a neighborhood in Lafayette, Indiana, USA. The date range is the second half of 2016 (left) and the first half of 2017 (right)

as a darkened hot spot in the right image in Fig. 3.3, relative to the left image. A numeric label at this address indicated that the number of 'Other Assault' increased from five to ten incidents between the two periods at the apartment complex in the lower left of each image.

Discussion

Insight into Crime Trends

The examples demonstrate how VALET can provide both officers and the public insight into surrounding crime trends only a laptop and an internet connection. In the community meetings, the initial query results guided the conversation between the officers and the attendees. For example, the instantaneous display of crime uptick led to the discussion about whether the attendees felt that the data accurately assessed changes in their neighborhood. Additionally, the reduction of 'Auto Law Violation' from 23 for the first half of 2016 to ten for the second half of 2016 could prompt the discussion of contributing factors to the downward trend, such as changes in police behavior, new street signs or traffic signals, or environmental factors like weather.

The change in the data itself does not explain causality, but identifying change can help determine the contributing factors. 'Other Assaults' rising to the most predominantly reported incident in the rank view led us to identify additional trends related to this incident type. The hot spots in Fig. 3.3 not only map the change in the distribution of 'Other Assaults,' but they pinpoint an address where twice as many incidents have been reported in the most recent 6-months span. The police and community members could use such information to evaluate and jointly determine factors at the location that have led to this increase. In doing so, the joint effort could take on a POP approach to address the core issue, such as a new tenant or change in management at the apartment, rather than focusing on reducing incidents.

Community Perception

Interactions from the three community meetings support that VALET can aid in community policing. The ability to answer community members questions with data in real time helped facilitate discussion. The observed conversations between the community and police was not a back and forth argument over perceived risks and actions, but rather a dialogue on ways to address problematic hot spots.

Furthermore, at the community meeting on June 20th, a majority of the attendees commended both LPD and VALET developers for jointly developing software for direct use at the community meetings. Such comments seemed to support a positive perception of the law enforcement agency. Additionally, a City Council Member in attendance at another community meeting asked for a follow-up to determine broader uses of VALET, further supporting the notion of multi-agency collaboration in POP.

Finally, the concept of hot spot policing may have been less controversial among the attendees because citizens had input in the decision-making process of patrol areas. Furthermore, community members now knew to be on the lookout for illicit activity at hot spot locations and that it was also their duty to inform the police of suspicious activity.

Limitations

First, the sample of attendees at the community meetings primarily represented an older and singular racial demographic. Although the group in attendance may have more positive views of the police, it may not extend to other segments of society. Second, we surveyed the use of VALET but did not conduct a controlled study to determine statistically significant changes in public perception. In future work, quantifying the impacts of real-time interactive and visual crime analytic software on perception may require a controlled study to compare groups with and without exposure to VALET. Third, although we captured temporal changes in crime incident data, we do not know whether these trends are fluctuations within the normal limits of the data. Additionally, we drew comparisons from data at only one period of one-half a year. Longer and shorter time bins may produce different results into crime trends and may provide additional insight.

Conclusion

We piloted VALET, an interactive spatiotemporal crime incident mapping software, as community outreach tool. Initial findings support that VALET can help Community Policing, Problem Oriented Policing, and increase understanding of the rationale behind Hot Spot Policing among community members that directly interact with officers and the software. The primary mechanism for the success of a crime incident visual analytic tool was real-time data exploration to address the questions and concerns of community members. Secondary mechanisms for success stemmed from community meeting attendees perceiving that they were working with the police, they had input in neighborhood policing, and the police were taking extra efforts of technology development for community policing.

Acknowledgement This work was partially funded by the by the U.S. Department of Homeland Security's VACCINE Center under Award Number 2009-ST-061-CI0003 and the European Commission under grant number H2020-FCT-2014 TRILLION, REA grant agreement number [653256].

References

Braga, A. A. (2001, 11). The effects of hot spots policing on crime. *The Annals of the American Academy of Political and Social Science, 578*, 104–125.
Braga, A. A. (2014). Problem-oriented policing. In *Encyclopedia of criminology and criminal justice* (pp. 3989–4000). New York: Springer New York. https://doi.org/10.1007/978-1-4614-5690-2_266.
Coquilhat, J. (2008). *Community policing: An international literature review*. Wellington: New Zealand Police Association Incorporated.
Forst, B. (2008). *Improving police effectiveness and transparency: National information needs on law enforcement* (Tech. Rep.). Washington, DC: Bureau of Justice Statistics.
Leitner, M., & Brecht, H. (2007, 5). Software review: Crime analysis and mapping with GeoDa 0.9.5-i. *Social Science Computer Review, 25*(2), 265–271. Retrieved from https://doi.org/10.1177/0894439307298921.
Levine, N. (2013). *CrimeStat IV – A spatial statistics program for the analysis of crime incident locations*. Washington, DC: National Institute of Justice.
Malik, A., Maciejewski, R., McCullough, S., Ebert, D. S., & Towers, S. (2014, 12). Proactive spatiotemporal resource allocation and predictive visual analytics for community policing and law enforcement. *IEEE Transactions on Visualization and Computer Graphics, 20*(12), 1863–1872.
Scheider, M. C., Rowell, T., & Bezdikian, V. (2003, 12). The impact of citizen perceptions of community policing on fear of crime: Findings from twelve cities. *Police Quarterly, 6*(4), 363–386. Retrieved from http://journals.sagepub.com/doi/10.1177/1098611102250697.
Trojanowicz, R. C., & Bucqueroux, B. (1990). *Community policing: A contemporary perspective*. Cincinnati: Anderson Pub.
Wang, G., Akers, A., de Queiroz Neto, J. F., Surakitbanharn, C., & Ebert, D. S. (2017). Spatiotemporal driven analysis of law enforcement data. In *The IEEE Visualization Workshop on Visualization in Practice*, IEEE Computer Society, 2017

Weisburd, D., & Eck, J. E. (2004). What can police do to reduce crime, disorder, and fear? *The Annals of the American Academy of Political and Social Science, 593*, 42–65. https://doi.org/10.2307/4127666.

Weisburd, D., Telep, C. W., Hinkle, J. C., & Eck, J. E. (2010, 2). Is problem-oriented policing effective in reducing crime and disorder? *Criminology & Public Policy, 9*(1), 139–172. Retrieved from http://doi.wiley.com/10.1111/j.1745-9133.2010.00617.x.

Weisburd, D. L., Groff, E. R., & Yang, S. M. (2012). *The criminology of place: Street segments and our understanding of the crime problem*. Oxford: Oxford University Press.

Chapter 4
Robust End-User-Driven Social Media Monitoring for Law Enforcement and Emergency Monitoring

Birgit Kirsch, Sven Giesselbach, David Knodt, and Stefan Rüping

Introduction

It has been widely proven that in case of emergencies and crisis situations content published on social media platforms, such as Twitter, constitutes a valuable source of information. As stated in Imran et al. (2015), Twitter has been used in various crisis scenarios to identify events, monitor event progress, summarize tweets to give a situational overview and classify them to extract relevant content. In this paper we propose a social media monitoring and analysis framework that provides support to the security sector and is based on the needs of two running H2020-projects in the area of community policing and emergency response, CITYCoP and E2MC.

CITYCoP, short for Citizen Interaction Technologies Yield Community Policing, aims at developing applications that facilitate community policing. One idea behind the project is to mine social media platforms to assess the perceived quality of life of the citizens.

The purpose of the **E2MC project**, short for Evolution of Emergency Copernicus services, is to extend the available Copernicus Emergency Management System (EMS) that provides an early warning and rapid mapping services in case of emergencies. By integrating an analysis platform capable of extracting crisis-related information from social media, the quality of the delivered information should be improved and the speed in which the affected area can be located and damage can be assessed should be increased. The main problem we face in both use cases is to flexibly adapt to new scenarios and provide an analysis pipeline that can be operated

B. Kirsch (✉) · S. Giesselbach · D. Knodt · S. Rüping
Fraunhofer Institute for Intelligent Analysis and Information Systems, Sankt Augustin, Germany
e-mail: birgit.kirsch@iais.fraunhofer.de; sven.giesselbach@iais.fraunhofer.de;
david.knodt@iais.fraunhofer.de; stefan.rueping@iais.fraunhofer.de

© The Author(s) 2018
G. Leventakis, M. R. Haberfeld (eds.), *Community-Oriented Policing and Technological Innovations*, SpringerBriefs in Criminology,
https://doi.org/10.1007/978-3-319-89294-8_4

by a user without expert knowledge in data analytics. In order to achieve this, we propose a framework that combines different machine learning approaches and can be enriched by user knowledge about the targeted event or location.

Related Work

A variety of methods have been applied to social media in the past in order to classify crisis-related tweets and to obtain useful information. One simple method is the keyword matching approach. In a predefined keyword dictionary, relevant words are collected. According to their appearance in a message text tweets can be extracted or classified (Olteanu et al. 2014). In more sophisticated approaches machine learning techniques are applied to develop models that are capable of automatically classifying tweets. These can be separated into supervised and unsupervised methods. Supervised methods learn models based on an already labeled dataset and can then be applied to incoming tweets. Caragea et al. (2016) and Nguyen et al. (2016) use online deep learning to classify tweets as informative or not informative. Nguyen et al. (2016) additionally partition crisis-related tweets into information-specific subclasses. Most of the frameworks proposed and developed in the context of event- and crisis-analysis, such as Tweedr (Ashktorab et al. 2014) or AIDR (Imran et al. 2014), are built upon these supervised techniques which rely on labeled datasets. We decided to integrate an unsupervised learning method that is able to train models without the need for a labeled set to overcome this drawback. To the best of our knowledge, there are only few examples in literature that follow this approach. Imran and Castillo (2015) use an unsupervised topic modeling technique, LDA, to generate candidate categories for tweet classifications. Kireyev et al. (2009) explore, how topics models can be used to analyze disaster-related Tweets. One reason why these techniques are not yet widely spread is that they uncover hidden structures that are not necessarily of interest for a user. Wang et al. (2016) present an extension of LDA, the Targeted Topic Model, that is capable of building topics around an aspect of interest. Based on this algorithm we propose an end-user driven approach to analyze tweets with respect to the location, relevant hashtags or sentiment.

System Overview

Our system contains the following components to process crawled Tweets: The **text processing component** applies typical text preprocessing techniques, such as sentence splitting, tokenization and stemming, to prepare the tweets for further analysis. The data is then enriched by integrating Hashtags, URL categories and handles as additional features. Furthermore, a user can define an event-profile with a georeference and the time the event started. Based on the profile, we calculate the distance of the tweets geolocation to the area of interest and the time elapsed since the event started. The **sentiment analysis component** identifies the polarity of texts in terms of whether the texts are emotionally positive, negative or neutral. This so called sentiment is added as an additional feature for the topic extraction component. The **topic extraction component** is the core step of our approach and will be described in detail in section "End-User-Driven Topic Detection". The **visualization component** is used to display enriched tweet data and enables the user to monitor tweets based on their location, derived sentiment and assigned topics. Tweets can be clustered based on their density and according to the assigned topics or keywords contained. Additionally, interactive filters based on keywords and topics can be applied to support specific scenarios.

End-User-Driven Topic Detection

Most text analytic models rely on a set of parameters or constraints that have to be set in advance of the model training. Since these parameters can heavily influence the model performance, this training process often requires complex tuning and expert data science knowledge. To allow a user to influence the analysis pipeline in a more natural way, we focus on an extension of the broadly used topic modeling algorithm LDA (Blei et al. 2003), the targeted topic model (Wang et al. 2016), that is capable of generating flexible models and integrating user domain knowledge about the event of interest.

LDA assumes that each document can be described as a mixture over topics, where each topic represents a distribution over words. A major problem one faces when applying LDA to analyze tweets is, that topics of interest may not be detected and the topics reflecting the dataset are to coarse. The idea of targeted topic modeling is to focus on an aspect the user is interested in by setting target keywords in advance. Based on this target a topic model is generated. This model consists of one major topic reflecting the content not related to the aspect and multiple fine-grained topics related to the aspect. The topics are represented as word distributions. By defining a set of target keywords related to an event of interest, these topic models can be used to extract tweets related to an event and to uncover useful structures to cluster these tweets. Figure 4.1 shows the analysis process compared to the baseline LDA-approach and a keyword based approach. In the keyword-based approach, a keyword list is used to filter relevant tweets while in the LDA approach, keyword lists are used to identify relevant topics by comparing them to the topic-word-distributions. In both scenarios, the selection of this keywords plays a crucial rule and heavily affects the quality of the retrieved content. The advantage of the targeted topic model is, that it automatically extends the keywords assumed to be relevant based on the input keyword list and the word co-occurrences in the tweets. This allows a more intuitive keyword selection without the need for expert refinement. To cover a rich spectrum of relevant information, we extend the model and enrich the input data with additional keywords representing different

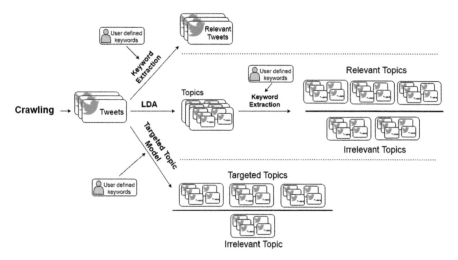

Fig. 4.1 Identification of relevant tweets

forms of information, such as the sentiment, the location and other meta data. We chose keywords as the way the information is exchanged, since it is easy to inspect and understand for the end-user and can be extended to other relevant types of information.

Experiments and Results

To evaluate our methods, we perform an experimental analysis of tweet data related to three crisis-events, the flood in Alberta in 2013, the Bombings in Boston during and after the marathon in April 2013 and the explosion at the West Fertilizer Company storage and distribution facility in April 2013. Therefore, we merged two publicly available datasets, CRISISLEX26 (Olteanu et al. 2015) and CRISISLEX6 (Olteanu et al. 2014) that were labeled from crowd-source workers as "on-topic" and "off-topic" and are assigned to one of six categories, e.g., "Infrastructure and utilities" and "Donations and volunteering". The label information assigned to each tweet is only used to evaluate the performance of the trained model. The analysis itself is performed on the unlabeled dataset. After preparation, we generated three datasets with around 10,000 tweets each. To evaluate our analysis approach on these dataset, we simulated an interactive analysis workflow that consists of three steps: The identification of event-related tweets, the identification and analysis of topic structures and the visual analysis.

Identification of event-related tweets: based on an input keyword set a targeted topic model is trained and applied to classify tweets as relevant or not relevant. To examine the robustness of the model, we pick very general and simple target

Table 4.1 Comparison of tweet-classification techniques

Model-type	Texas explosion			Boston bombing			Alberta flood		
	Precision	Recall	FMeas.	Precision	Recall	FMeas.	Precision	Recall	FMeas.
Targeted TM	0.973	0.835	**0.900**	0.938	**0.698**	**0.800**	0.937	**0.980**	0.958
LDA	0.817	**0.903**	0.858	0.816	0.589	0.684	0.812	0.901	0.854
Keyword	**0.995**	0.796	0.885	**0.959**	0.660	0.782	**0.957**	0.976	**0.977**

Table 4.2 Top 20 words for the identified sub-categories

Infrastructure damage:
Bowriver, downtown, emerg, calgari, bridg, update, medicinhat, state, local, remain, citi, power, rcmp, water, school, close, canmor, break, expect, elbow
Donations:
Relief, donat, love, redcross, great, text, peopl, victim, find, made, good, feel, affect, bad, provid, send, pretti, assist, custom, fan

keywords for model training and the keyword matching. For the Alberta Flood the target keywords are set to all words matching the substring "flood", for the explosion in Texas we pick all words matching the substring "explo" and the substrings to identify the Boston event are "bomb" and "marathon". To assess the performance of the model, the results are compared to two different baseline-approaches:

- a keyword matching based approach, in which tweets are filtered as relevant when they contain a word in the specified keyword set.
- the direct application of LDA, where each tweet assigned to a topic identified as crisis-related is treated as relevant. We assumed all topics with high word probability for the words listed in the defined keyword set to be crisis-related.

Table 4.1 shows the performance for each approach. In all three datasets the targeted topic model outperforms the baseline LDA regarding F1 score. In the Alberta dataset, the identification seems to be not that challenging and the use of the targeted topic model approach cannot improve the performance. One reason could be that most of the tweets contain flood-related hashtags, such as #albertaflood or #abflood.

Identification and analysis of topic structures: In the next phase we further analyze the learned topic-word-distribution. In the experiment, we focused on the Alberta dataset and chose a model that consists of 25 topics describing the different hidden structures in the event-related tweets and one major topic assigned to all tweets identified as not event-related. In order to focus on a specific aspect of interest, we concentrate on the topics best matching manually defined keywords, in this case "blocked / closed / damaged" for damage related topics and "donate / fund / relief" for donation related topics. The results are presented in Table 4.2. The damage-focused topics not only contain words describing infrastructure, such as road, school or bridge, but are also capable of uncovering affected rivers, e.g. the Elbow River or affected towns, such as Medicine Hat, and damaged areas, such as the Bowness Park.

Table 4.3 Meta features with high relevance in the damage related and donation related topics

Handles		Hashtags		Sentiment	
Damage	Donation	Damage	Donation	Damage	Donation
Nenshi	redcrosscanada	#yycflood	#abflood	Neutral 67%	Neutral 65%
Calgary police	Mookalicious	#nature	#yycflood	Negative 18%	Positive 19%
Calgary herald	redcrossab	#abflood	#yychelps	Positive 15%	Negative 16 %
City of calgary	westjet	#yyc	#canmore		
Druh farrel	premier_redford	#CHLive	#medhat	Distance	
Weather network	wbrettwilson	#stampede	#mhflood	Damage	Donation
Mookalicious	nateinvegas	#flames	#heartbreaking	−100 km 100%	1000 km + 39.5%
Carrie tait	starbucks	#sunnyside	#disgusted		100 km − 28.5%
CalgaryPolice	cityofcalgary	#UCalgary	#shame		1000 km − 20.5%
globeandmail	yychelps	#staysafe	#blackhawk		5000 km + 11.5%

Next, the meta features assigned to the topics are examined. Table 4.3 lists the handles, locations, hashtags, time and URLs related to damage- or donation-topics. While in the damage-related topics the fact, that a tweet position is close to the event, is very relevant, in the donation topic this is not that important. The detected URLs as well as the handles and hashtags for the donation-topic mainly focus on institutions offering help, such as the Red Cross and politicians providing support. In the damage-related topics the focus is set to news agencies, the police and the affected towns.

Visual Analysis: To obtain a better insight, we visually examine the trained topic model. Therefore, a sentiment-map is generated, showing all tweets near Alberta assigned to the damage- or the donation-topic colored with the sentiment (Fig. 4.2). In the area very close to the affected area, the sentiment mainly seems to be negative in both topics. In the surrounding areas, there are more positive tweets contained in the donation topic. Next, the density based clusters for the tweets related to damage and the tweets related to donation are generated and analyzed to uncover topic hot spots. As we infer the user's location if the tweet location is not available, this clusters are influenced by the fact that all user tweets from a city are mapped to the same spot retrieved by the OpenStreetMap API. Nonetheless, this clustering can be an indicator for topic hot spots. By examining the hot spots for damage-related topics in the affected area, we could find useful information about the situation on side regarding power supply, bridge closures and pictures of flooded areas.

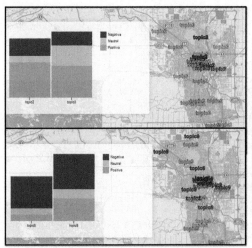 

Fig. 4.2 Left: Sentiment map for tweets assigned to the damage-topics (bottom) and donation-topics (top). Right: Identified damage-cluster near the elbow river

Conclusions

In this paper, we propose a robust framework that monitors and analyzes streams from social media and is adaptable by the end-user without the need for complex tuning. The system is based on state-of-the-art text mining technologies, including a convolutional neural network for sentiment detection and an extension of the Latent Dirichlet Allocation functionality to identify latent topics from tweets. Identified topics or relevant keywords are visualized on a map together with their respective sentiment. We processed the text and enriched it with several meta features, such as the location to be able to extract different information types during the analysis and set the analysis focus to different aspects.

Acknowledgements The first author has received funding from the European Unions Horizon 2020 research and innovation programme under grant agreement No 730082. The second author has received funding from the European Unions Horizon 2020 research and innovation programme under grant agreement No 653811.

References

Ashktorab, Z., Brown, C., Nandi, M., & Culotta, A. (2014). Tweedr: Mining twitter to inform disaster response. In *Iscram*, Toulouse.

Blei, D. M., Ng, A. Y., Jordan, M. I., & Lafferty, J. (2003). Latent dirichlet allocation. *The Journal of Machine Learning Research, 3*, 993–1022.

Caragea, C., Silvescu, A., & Tapia, A. H. (2016). Identifying informative messages in disaster events using convolutional neural networks. In *International Conference on Information Systems for Crisis Response and Management*.

Imran, M., & Castillo, C. (2015). Towards a data-driven approach to identify crisisrelated topics in social media streams. In *Proceeding of the 24th International Conference on World Wide Web* (pp. 1205–1210). New York: ACM. Retrieved from http://doi.org/10.1145/2740908.2741729

Imran, M., Castillo, C., Lucas, J., Meier, P., & Vieweg, S. (2014). AIDR: Artificial intelligence for disaster response. In *Proceedings of the 23rd International Conference on World Wide Web* (pp. 159–162). New York: ACM. Retrieved from http://doi.org/10.1145/2567948.2577034

Imran, M., Castillo, C., Diaz, F., & Vieweg, S. (2015). Processing social media messages in mass emergency: A survey. *ACM Computing Surveys 47*(4). https://doi.org/10.1145/2771588

Kireyev, K., Palen, L., & Anderson, K. (2009). Applications of topics models to analysis of disaster-related twitter data, 11 Dec 2009.

Nguyen, D. T., Joty, S. R., Imran, M., Sajjad, H., & Mitra, P. (2016). Applications of online deep learning for crisis response using social media information. CoRR, abs/1610.01030. Retrieved from http://arxiv.org/abs/1610.01030

Olteanu, A., Castillo, C., Diaz, F., & Vieweg, S. (2014). Crisislex: A lexicon for collecting and filtering microblogged communications in crises. In *International AAAI Conference on Web and Social Media*. Retrieved from http://www.aaai.org/ocs/index.php/ICWSM/ICWSM14/paper/view/8091

Olteanu, A., Vieweg, S., & Castillo, C. (2015). What to expect when the unexpected happens: Social media communications across crises. In *Proceedings of the 18th ACM Conference on Computer Supported Cooperative Work & Social Computing* (pp. 994–1009). New York: ACM. Retrieved from http://doi.acm.org/10.1145/2675133.2675242

Wang, S., Chen, Z., Fei, G., Liu, B., & Emery, S. (2016). Targeted topic modeling for focused analysis. In *Proceedings of the 22nd ACM SIGKDD International Conference on Knowledge Discovery and Data Mining – KDD'16* (pp. 1235–1244). Retrieved from http://dl.acm.org/citation.cfm?doid=2939672.2939743

Chapter 5
Architecting Next Generating Community Policing Solutions

Gohar Sargsyan, Raymond Binnendijk, and Eltjo Poort

Emerging Trends for Next Generation Community Policing and INSPEC²T

"Community Policing" is a strategy of policing that focuses on police building ties and working closely with members of the communities. With the police innovation, the technology advancement, growing data and need of ore complex and advanced analytics, new ways of collaboration between communities and Law Enforcement Agencies (LEA) is needed. "Next Generation Community Policing" (NGCP) introduces this these new ways, which aims at seamless collaboration between police and communities considering also aspects such as Societal, Ethical, Legal & Data Privacy, Criminology and Technological Applications related to the Geographic Information Systems, Smart Apps and integrated Networks.

The INSPEC²T project is a next generation community policing research and innovation project. INSPEC²T project (**I**nspiring Citize**NS** **P**articipation for **E**nhanced **C**ommunity Poli**C**ing Ac**T**ions (http://inspec2t-project.eu/en/) project is funded by the European Commission, under the "H2020-FCT-2014 Ethical/Societal Dimension Topic 2: Enhancing cooperation between law enforcement agencies and citizens – Community policing" call. The INSPEC²T projects' scope is to develop a sustainable framework for Community Policing that effectively addresses and promotes seamless collaboration between the police and the community. In order to encompass the variety of European police cultures and contemporary experiences of police reform the consortium consists of eighteen partners from eight European countries (http://inspec2t-project.eu/en/partners-2). It consists of

G. Sargsyan (✉) · R. Binnendijk · E. Poort
CGI Group Inc., Rotterdam, The Netherlands
e-mail: gohar.sargsyan@cgi.com; raymond.binnendijk@cgi.com; eltjo.poort@cgi.com

© The Author(s) 2018   37
G. Leventakis, M. R. Haberfeld (eds.), *Community-Oriented Policing and Technological Innovations*, SpringerBriefs in Criminology,
https://doi.org/10.1007/978-3-319-89294-8_5

18 partners covering research, academia, business, non-profit and government organizations from 8 European countries and 45 more high level experts and stakeholder advisory group members coming from the worldwide. The INSPEC^{2}T project consists of eight Work Packages (WP's (http://inspec2t-project.eu/en/work-breakdown)), covering various aspects of the problem domain. A number of these WP's are related to the realization of an actual working IT-system. In 2017, this system is being demonstrated and validated in five EU cities (Valencia, Belfast, Engomi, Preston and Groningen) by relevant stakeholders in two phases.

This paper gives an overview of the architectural work done, led by CGI, supported by and in close collaboration with various consortium partners.

Architecture Work Package

Within INSPEC^{2}T, Work Package 3 (WP3) is responsible for architecture, which constitutes the central work package of the INSPEC^{2}T project. Through it the societal and functional requirements, defined in WP1 and WP2, are translated into technology, beyond the state of the art solutions, to be implemented in WP4.

The INSPEC^{2}T architecture process has taken place partly in parallel with the work on functional and non-functional requirements in Work Packages WP1 and WP2. This has allowed the architecture and requirements processes to mutually benefit from each other's progress, and resulted in cohesion between requirements and architecture.

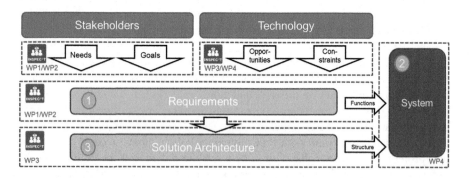

The figure shows how WP3 is positioned among the other WPs. As indicated by the green numbers, architecture work consists of:

1. Making sure system requirements are clear, high-quality, feasible and "ready-for-consumption" for the system development (WP4).
2. Making sure all significant aspects are sufficiently covered, the architecture is aligned with the various technical opportunities and constraints and "technical partners" (the partners which are qualified for technological and technical expertise) are fully aligned and can hit the ground running when starting WP4.
3. Shaping the architecture.

Risk and Cost Driven Architecture

The architecture approach followed in INSPEC^{2}T is CGI's Risk- and Cost-Driven (RCDA (Poort E./CGI), which is recognized in the Open Group Certified Architect program. RCDA was developed to close the gaps between enterprise and software architecture.

Existing software architecture practices often are too limited in scope for the solutions that need to be architected. However, enterprise architecture practices are too heavy for the agility required to manage time pressures and frequently occurring changes and uncertainty. RCDA incorporates a number of aspects from agile software development practices, such as the use of a backlog of architectural concerns, to be frequently reprioritized based on economic factors like risk and cost.

During the INSPEC^{2}T system architecture design, RCDA method supported the architects throughout the process of interpreting stakeholders' requirements, and subsequently designing and delivering the best fitting solution in a lean, mean and agile manner. Architectural concerns and architectural decisions are weighed throughout the process, and stakeholder requirements are constantly taken into account (Poort and van Vliet 2012).

The figure below describes the architectural design process:

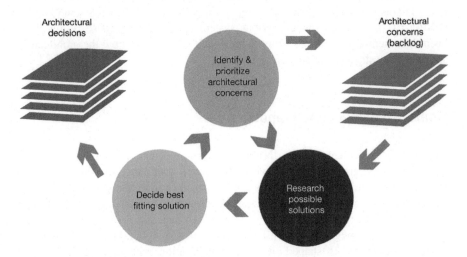

When viewed as a risk and cost management discipline, architecture does not need to obstruct agility. RCDA offers a proven approach to solution architecture that is well-suited to today's agile end-users needs which is the base for INSPEC^{2}T.

Applying the RCDA method, setting up the INSPEC^{2}T architecture different practice sets are identified (requirement analysis, solution shaping, architecture validation and architecture fulfilment).

The application of RCDA brings various advantages to INSPEC^{2}T:

- It **smoothens communication** between solution architects and business stake-holders – RCDA-trained architects communicate about architectural decisions and trade-offs.
- A **clear and agreed set of architectural requirements** for design decisions, using objective and economically oriented trade-offs, rather than hypes or personal preferences.
- It reduces the risk of **delayed delivery and budget overruns** – RCDA sees architecture as a risk- and cost management discipline with economic awareness in the design process and avoiding "gold-plating".
- It **enhances the quality of solutions** – RCDA practices are CMMI (Capability Maturity Model Integration) compliant, and contain guidance for early and effective evaluation of quality attributes.
- It **creates transparency in costing structures** – RCDA provides traceability from architectural requirements to the costing model for the whole solution and its parts.

According to RCDA principles, the architecture work starts with identifying architectural concerns with the highest impact in terms of risk and cost, and addressing those concerns by making architectural decisions. Hence, the architecture contains the results of the most impactful architectural decisions made in the INSPEC^{2}T project and related various system requirements. These results have been documented in multiple *views*, where each view shows how the architecture addresses key stakeholder concerns.

Goals, Challenges and Opportunities

During the implementation of INSPEC^{2}T system design and architecture, the project partners agreed on the following approach: to facilitate a successful commu-nity policing solution the architecture should provide a foundation for an IT-system capable of connecting police and citizens (bi-directional). Enabling, managing and exploiting an information overload is another key success factor. In addition, the system has to be integratable in various, continually changing, IT-environments.

The architecture is shaped in close collaboration with eight EU technical partners. Each partner brings specific expertise (being brainpower and software products) to the project. Forging these building blocks together, leveraging and integrating the software and facilitating efficient collaboration, is both the primary challenge and a major opportunity to be addressed.

The INSPEC^{2}T project's work packages are primarily positioned sequentially (albeit partly overlapping and with some iterations included). This classical approach brings important structure to the project, but also reduces agility and the opportunity for including learning cycles.

Development Approach

We addressed these concerns by **communication continually** during weekly WebEx meetings, organizing an early physical meeting between technical partners, and creating a **collaboration platform** Content Management System (CMS) where the emerging architectural decisions and views were shared with all technical partners. These steps allowed us to quickly converge on an architecture. This **architecture** (elaborated on more later in this article) **allows for an incremental and iterative delivery strategy** of which an initial description was provided.

WP4 in INSPEC^{2}T project work-plan is responsible for implementation of INSPEC^{2}T system, as designed in WP3, developing also all back-end modules, by integrating prior implemented components, thus delivering it as a usable platform for performing the pilots. As part of the architecture delivery view a **development approach** was provided to develop or otherwise obtain the deliverable elements that make up the technical solution. This approach is being used by all technical partners during the execution of WP4 tasks directly related to a shared integrated environment. Each technical partner is free to decide on its local development approach.

The development of the integrated INSPEC^{2}T components is a continuous process which will contain all the required steps to assure quality during the entire lifetime of the project. This process can be represented as a virtual circle that contains the following functional components:

1. Source-code-versioning and management,
2. Continuous integration,
3. Quality assurance of generated code,
4. Builds (a.k.a. artefacts) management,
5. Issue tracking.

Each part of the circle is supported by mature pre-setup tools that interoperate smoothly. The tooling is part of the **central Integration test environment** provided by one of the technical partners.

Integration Guidelines

To furthermore address the concern of integration it's crucial to get the interfaces right (*focus on what's going on between the boxes*). This is why the architecture includes **interfaces guidelines**. Each technical partner should design and build its interfaces following these guidelines, or explicitly explain why a guideline is violated. These guidelines are:

1. Use REST (https://en.wikipedia.org/wiki/Representational_state_transfer).
2. Asynchronous chunky (not chatty) dialogs between components to promote loosely coupling and reduce overall bandwidth use.
3. Interfaces should abstract the underlying service complexities. Naming is semantic (not just CRUD (https://en.wikipedia.org/wiki/Create,_read,_update_and_delete) and thereby easy to understand by humans.
4. Transport big chunks of data using references. But no integration over shared databases.
5. Use choreography over orchestration for managing business process communication logic.
6. Avoid big bang breaking of interfaces by potentially supporting (two) coexisting interface versions.
7. Adapt Continuous Integration, as a crucial practice in securing successful integration.

Integration Plan

The development approach and interfacing guidelines provide technical partners guidance in "how" to develop and integrate their various components. In addition, the architecture provides guidance in "what" to develop, focusing on developing, deploying and integrating software components early and often, making sure the important (high impact on Risks or Costs) stuff is covered first. This guidance is provided via an **integration plan**, comprised of the following steps:

1. **Setup Integrated Test Environment**
   The central test environment, including tools support.
2. **UI Mock-up**
   Mock-ups of the UI components will look like the real thing, but will not do useful work beyond what the user sees. Mock-ups are used to discuss requirements and GUI/design-ideas.

3. **Interface Exemplar**
   Working code examples will help to understand written documents better. Start delivering a first draft version of an INSPEC^{2}T service focusing on implementing the interfaces, following the interface guidelines above. This service will be a real-world template for future services to be built by the other technical partners and will be part of and the starting point for the architectural prototype.

4. **Architectural Prototype**
   The INSPEC^{2}T prototype is built using all or the majority of INSPEC^{2}T components integrated and aligned with the architecture. The goal is to validate the architecture as early as possible. The prototype will be based on working software containing basic and preliminary functionality.

5. **Initial Version**
   A first version of the INSPEC^{2}T consisting of all INSPEC^{2}T components delivering at least all mandatory requirements. This version will be used for and will also be improved during system integration and technical testing.

6. **Pilots**
   During five test-case pilots INSPEC^{2}T used and validated in a real-life environment. Each pilot city will have a dedicated hosting environment and if needed a custom version of the INSPEC^{2}T system being a subset of the initial version and/or a configured version. Feedback from the various pilots will be consolidated and used to improve the INSPEC^{2}T system.

Steps 1, 2, 3 and 4 are part of WP3. This means the installation of environments, validation of the architecture and development and delivery of (preliminary versions of) the system already started during the architecture phase.

Open, Modular and Loosely Coupled Architecture

So, guidelines and steps, at the end of the day architecture is all about IT-system design. For Next Generation Community Policing the architecture should primarily address bi-directional information flow between people and systems and dealing with potentially large, changing and various flows of data. And last but not least, the architecture should facilitate flexible integration in a continually changing IT-landscape.

An open, modular and loosely coupled architecture meets these requirements.

This architecture is documented via a set of multiple views. The view below visualizes how components are loosely intercoupled dealing with information flowing through the system.

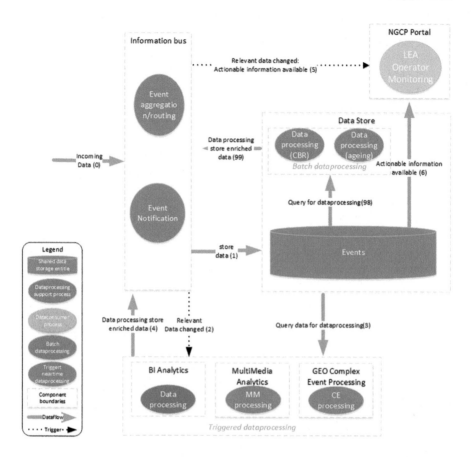

Incoming data is channelled through the information bus and stored centrally.

A **generic meta-data domain model** is in place as the base for data storage, transportation and message exchange schema's.

To provide more decoupling and modifiability a **choreographed** (instead of orchestrated), **publish/subscribe** design is used. This means the business process logic is not centralized but instead individual data processing components know what will trigger their data processing process. This way, if data processing components need to be added or removed they can just (un-)subscribe. No direct dependencies between data processing components and no need for code or configuration changes to a central component.

The various components are **connected loosely**, via **REST** interfaces.

Each component preferably is hosted using **virtual machines**, making physical **deployment flexible** and enhances **scalability**.

Architecture Validation Approach

Referring to the chapter "Integration plan", steps 1, 2, 3, 4 and 5 were demonstrated and validated within WP3 during the stakeholders advisory group and external expert group's meeting of the INSPEC^{2}T project on April 19, 2016. The system's rapid prototype has been demonstrated: after UI mock up presentations and architecture prototype demonstration, a questionnaire was offered to the senior LEA, Government and Community representatives to validate the architecture to allow us to move forward with the development of the system.

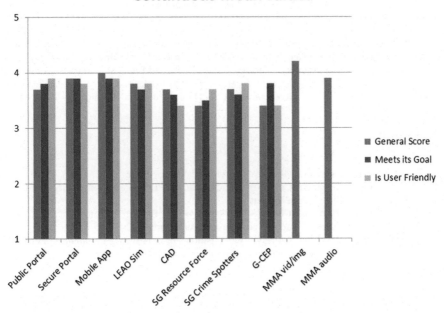

As illustrated in Figure, the rapid prototype validation containing all modules has been validated by the senior end-users, who are the project's (Stakeholder Advisory Board (SAG) / External Expert Group (EEG) members. For the criteria "General Score", 1 is low, or a bad score, and 5 is high, or a perfect score. For the criteria "Meets its Goal" and "Is User Friendly" selecting 1 means "Totally Disagree" and selecting 5 means "Totally Agree" (NSPEC^{2}T project's deliverable – D3.4 – 2nd SAG Report). Although overall assessment had positive scores,, however improvements and suggestions were provided which were taken on board for the development.

After the development of the system the Step 6 was conducted to validate the system during each of the 5 pilots in two phases. It is important to note, that the conclusion was that the architecture was solid and no breaks have been identified.

Designed for Integration and Evolution, More than a Set of Views

Architecture in today's world is not just about drawing a set of views, aimed to address current requirements. A sustainable NGCP-solution should be able to integrate in numerous heterogeneous environments and evolve over time. This is facilitated by an open, modular and loosely coupled ecosystem, designed in close collaboration with the various expert partners.

Acknowledgements This paper is based on the collaborative work conducted within the project INSPEC2T, the CGI's already existing practices and experience and the authors' vision on the subject. Having central role in setting up the framework (tools, architecture and methodologies) of the INSPEC^{2}T system, as part of the joint work plan, the authors received essential input from technical partners on the components under their development or their central development role, other partners with other valuable input which made the work complete. In particular, the authors would like to thank the following individuals and project partners: INTRASOFT – Sofia TSEKERIDOU, and Dane Vergeti, ADITESS –Elisavet Charalambous, Nikos Koutras, VICOMTECH – Peter Leskovsky, Santiago Prieto Calero, SATWAYS – Antonis Kostaridis, Leonidas Perlepes, KEMEA – George Leventakis, George Kokkinis, George Papalandrapolos, IMC – Spyros Tzavellas, Panos Georgolios, EXUS – Dimitris Katsaros, PLAYGEN – Kam Star.

References

CRUD. https://en.wikipedia.org/wiki/Create,_read,_update_and_delete

INSPEC^{2}T project (Inspiring Citize**NS** **P**articipation for **E**nhanced **C**ommunity PoliCing AcTions). http://inspec2t-project.eu/en/

INSPEC^{2}T project (Inspiring Citize**NS** **P**articipation for **E**nhanced **C**ommunity PoliCing AcTions). *Project partners.* http://inspec2t-project.eu/en/partners-2

INSPEC^{2}T project (Inspiring Citize**NS** **P**articipation for **E**nhanced **C**ommunity PoliCing AcTions). *Work breakdown.* http://inspec2t-project.eu/en/work-breakdown

Poort, E., & CGI. *RCDA: Risk- and cost- driven architecture: Solution architecture for the agile age.* http://www.cs.vu.nl/~hans/publications/y2012/JSS-RCDA.pdf

Poort, E., & van Vliet, H. (2012). *RCDA: Architecting as a risk- and cost management discipline.* https://www.cgi.com/sites/default/files/white-papers/risk-and-cost-driven-architecture.pdf

REST – Representational State Transfer. https://en.wikipedia.org/wiki/Representational_state_transfer

Chapter 6
Developing and Assessing Next Generation Community Policing Social Networks with THOR Methodology

George Leventakis and George Kokkinis

Evolving Community Policing Models and the Impact of Social Network

Community Policing (CP) is built on the belief that people deserve and have a right "to have a say" in policing in exchange for their participation and support (Kenney and McNamara 1999). CP is "The process of enabling the participation of citizens and communities in policing at their chosen level, ranging from providing information and reassurance, to empowering them to identify and implement solutions to local problems and influence strategic priorities and decisions" (Trottier 2015).

CP has become the paradigm of contemporary policing, evolving significantly over the past years (Johnston 2005; Tilley 2008). The CP evolution initiated with 1st Generation and "Innovation" (1979–1986) where early CP initiatives were referenced as "experiments" and "demonstration projects". From 1987 to 1994 CP continued evolving with the "Diffusion" phase and focused on drugs and fear of crime issues. The third generation known as "Institutionalization" continues from 1995 up to date with a broader scope of CP activities (Peak 2013).

Nowadays, a major difference to the classic CP studies of Whyte (1943), Gans (1982) and others is the emergence and spread of social media networks and mobile internet devices. Manning (2011) recognized the importance of technological components (modules) in a police-designed Social Network required to serve the police needs and support crime mapping and analysis. In addition, the rise of virtual communities and 'horizontal' online social networks have complicated the

G. Leventakis (✉) · G. Kokkinis
Senior Advisor – European Projects, Center for Security Studies – KEMEA Hellenic Ministry of Interior – Public Order Sector, Athens, Greece
e-mail: gleventakis@kemea.gr; g.kokkinis@kemea-research.gr

© The Author(s) 2018   47
G. Leventakis, M. R. Haberfeld (eds.), *Community-Oriented Policing and Technological Innovations*, SpringerBriefs in Criminology,
https://doi.org/10.1007/978-3-319-89294-8_6

relationships with current police structures, which are organised geographically and hierarchically. Against the background of cultural and ethnic diversity the spread of new technologies injects an element of homogeneity and seemingly a level playing field. Therefore, the implementation of social media modules should be exploited by the police as a channel to establish interaction with community members.

Next Generation Community Policing: The INSPEC^{2}T Solution

INSPEC^{2}T,[1] is a 3-year EU project started in May 2015, and has already mobilised and engaged a critical mass of users, across EU and overseas. With special emphasis on social media use in CP, it consolidates and modernises bidirectional communication of stakeholders, using multi-level anonymity flags.

The projects' scope is to develop a sustainable framework for CP that effectively addresses and promotes seamless collaboration between the police and various communities. The fundamental goal of the project is to validate the research results and to identify good practices on cooperation between police and the society at a local, regional and national level. This concept includes incident reporting from both registered and anonymous community members using a properly designed social network for CP. The reports are processed online in a system made from intelligence components, which supports bidirectional and personalized communications, allow the engagement of community members to provide additional information and to enhance the use of available police resources. The concept described above is shown in Figs. 6.1 and 6.2.

INSPEC^{2}T Solution Modules

A modern CP solution should possess intelligence capabilities and its architecture has to be modular and based on open standard interfaces. This means that existing analysis modules and databases will be utilized and will be part of the advanced CP ecosystem. The INSPEC^{2}T advanced CP solution includes reporting tools, awareness raising & educational gaming apps as well as intelligent command & control modules.

Mobile Applications and Public Portal Two different incident reporting methods are supported. Citizens can either submit reports to the Public Portal using a computer or smartphone (without the installation of any application), or by installing the INSPEC^{2}T mobile application on their smartphones/tablets. An extended, in

---

[1] http://cordis.europa.eu/project/rcn/194895_en.html

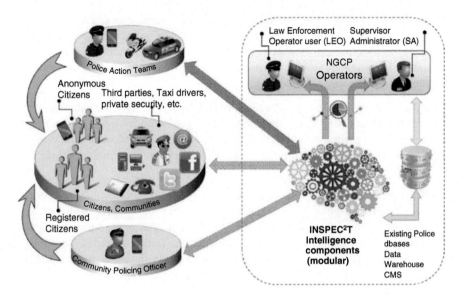

Fig. 6.1 The INSPEC^{2}T concept

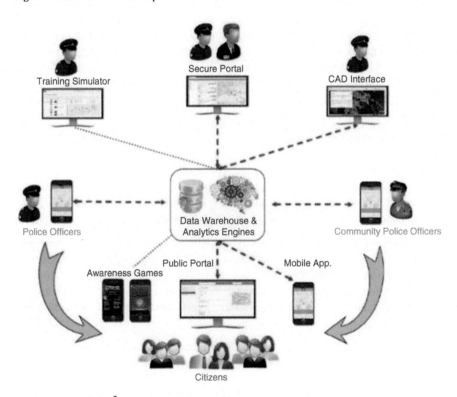

Fig. 6.2 The INSPEC^{2}T solution components

terms of functionalities, version of the mobile application is available to CP officers for managing the reports and interact further with the system and its operators. Apart of the Mobile Applications and the Public Portal, an awareness game is also available. The gaming module, Resource Force[2] aims to raise awareness about the citizens' contribution-value to CP.

Geospatial Complex Event Processing (GCEP) This module addresses the challenge of processing huge amounts of data generated by either registered or anonymous users with embedded geolocation information. The submitted datasets are processed and analysed in a structural manner to provide meaningful information.

Multimedia Analytics (MMA) module is capable of extracting semantic information from a wide range of multimedia data sources like text, images, audio streams and videos. The quality assurance of the MMA module allows pre-processing and discarding of low quality data. The valid data are further analysed to produce speech transcription, detect acoustic events, allow person/face detection and re-identification and perform other multimedia correlations.

Business Intelligence Analytics (BIA) is a module to: (i) compute metrics for the activity and engagement of both citizens and police from all CP communication channels (e.g. community forums, social media accounts, etc.), (ii) implement sentiment analysis for the messages exchanged in the above-named channels, (iii) build a rating based user profile, by computing each user's activity within the advanced CP – Social Network, which typifies how active the user is and if they are contributing helpful information to the system or if they are malicious. It has to be noted, however, that the rating essentially concerns the information provided by the user rather than the users themselves.

Case Based Reasoning (CBR) module consists, by design, of two different submodules. The first one is composed of rules that the user should adjust or modify to make use of expert knowledge. The second submodule is equipped with a knowledge base to enable the inference of new rules and actions based on previous knowledge. In essence, the CBR module implements a way to measure similarity between concepts and relations of a prevailing ontology.

Data Processing Ageing (DPA) has to be configured according to the corresponding regulatory frameworks. Records may only be stored following a legitimate reason and massive storage of preventive data is not allowed. Record lifetime and criteria for deletion have to be determined in accordance to Data Protection legislation. The renewal of an item's date of expiration is possible and needs to be initiated from a user with the appropriate access rights.

Data Warehouse (DWH) integrates data from multiple heterogeneous sources and in different formats to support analytical reporting, structured and/or ad hoc queries

---

[2]https://play.google.com/store/apps/details?id=com.playgen.ResourceForce

and decision making. DWH is an architectural model designed to support the flow of data from operational modules to decision support systems. The large amounts of heterogeneous data provided by citizens and communities over time are arranged into abstracted subject areas with time-variant versions of the same records, with an appropriate level of data grain or detail to make it useful for the intelligent modules described above to retrieve and analyse them.

Secure Portal (SP) The intelligence sub-modules mentioned above, (GCEP, MMA, BIA, CBR, DPA, and DWH) are all interfaced to the SP which provide operators with an advanced operational picture. The Law Enforcement Operator (LEO) and the INSPEC^{2}T Supervisor Administrator are in control of all CP submitted reports and, by utilising the intelligent processing capabilities of the advanced CP system, they manage all the reported incidents to extract useful and actionable information.

Training Simulator This module offers realistic in-situ simulations to allow the system administrators and Secure Portal operators to get familiarized with the platform, experience the potential impact of their decisions, interact in a safe environment, analyse their approach, facilitate peer assessment and benchmark so as to enable self-reflection and improvement. Moreover, the inclusion of courses with focus on privacy, data protection and how the system administrators should comply with ethical & legal and societal requirements are mandatory items included in the advanced offered CP training program.

Next Generation CP (NGCP) Functions Associated with Use Cases

A Use Case[3] is a list of actions, typically defining the interactions between an actor and a system, to achieve an outcome. They document step by step instructions how to test the built-in functionality and demonstrate specific features and functionalities of a Next Generation Community Policing – Social Network (NGCP-SN). The use case categories outline the interactions between members of a NGCP-SN first among themselves, and then with other (existing) social networks and finally describe the collaboration between community members and police officers. The Use Case categories include: (i) Interaction with NGCP-SN; (ii) Communities; (iii) Incident Reporting and Management; (iv) Interaction with other SN's; (v) Backend Intelligence; (vi) Rules and Supporting Actions. The above classification is illustrated in Fig. 6.3. Next are briefly described the above six use case categories.

---

[3]https://www.ibm.com/support/knowledgecenter/en/SSWSR9_11.0.0/com.ibm.pim.dev.doc/pim_tsk_arc_definingusecases.html

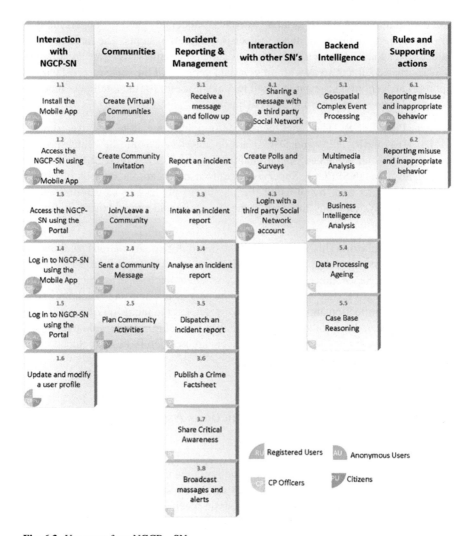

Interaction with NGCP-SN	Communities	Incident Reporting & Management	Interaction with other SN's	Backend Intelligence	Rules and Supporting actions
1.1 Install the Mobile App	2.1 Create (Virtual) Communities	3.1 Receive a message and follow up	4.1 Sharing a message with a third party Social Network	5.1 Geospatial Complex Event Processing	6.1 Reporting misuse and inappropriate behavior
1.2 Access the NGCP-SN using the Mobile App	2.2 Create Community Invitation	3.2 Report an incident	4.2 Create Polls and Surveys	5.2 Multimedia Analysis	6.2 Reporting misuse and inappropriate behavior
1.3 Access the NGCP-SN using the Portal	2.3 Join/Leave a Community	3.3 Intake an incident report	4.3 Login with a third party Social Network account	5.3 Business Intelligence Analysis	
1.4 Log in to NGCP-SN using the Mobile App	2.4 Sent a Community Message	3.4 Analyse an incident report		5.4 Data Processing Ageing	
1.5 Log in to NGCP-SN using the Portal	2.5 Plan Community Activities	3.5 Dispatch an incident report		5.5 Case Base Reasoning	
1.6 Update and modify a user profile		3.6 Publish a Crime Factsheet			
		3.7 Share Critical Awareness			
		3.8 Broadcast massages and alerts			

Registered Users   Anonymous Users

CP Officers   Citizens

Fig. 6.3 Use cases for a NGCP – SN

Interaction with NGCP-SN

There are three different types of users supported in the INSPEC^{2}T solution. These are *citizens* (*registered* and/or *anonymous*) who wish to interact with the NGCP-SN and *users with elevated access rights* like CP officers, neighbourhood watch group representatives and municipality personnel. The citizens are offered the following two options: a) interact with the system (two-way communications) by providing their contact details, and b) receive only alerts and notification (one-way communication) if they choose to remain anonymous. Both registered and anonymous users should be allowed to access a NGCP-SN and should be offered the same rights for crime reporting and receive information about CP activities, police reports, alerts, etc. A registered user is also allowed to provide information anonymously.

Users who wish to engage with the INSPEC^{2}T solution and interact with the system using their mobile device(s), should download the Mobile App[4] from their mobile applications store. The participants should be able to access the system also from the public portal using the browser in their mobile device. The users should be able to access the system either as registered and/or anonymous users.

Communities

The INSPEC^{2}T users should be able to form closed groups (communities) to discuss their safety and security needs and various topics of CP interest. There are two distinct categories of communities: Physical, where users are living in the same area will use the forum to exchange their views about crime / security in their neighbourhood or plan certain physically team activities; Virtual, where users with common interests (e.g. a merchant association) will come together to exchange ideas from their professional point of view. Following the creation of a community, it's members should send invitation to other users to join in. The created communities can also be announced in other SN's.

The community members should be able to post messages to other member(s) (one to one and one to many communication), or post messages to communities (one to all communications). The communication exchange can take place either publicly (message can be seen by other users at a later time) or privately within a group. Also, a group of LEAs assigned with CP duties should be reached either privately or publicly.

Incident Reporting and Management

Both registered and anonymous participants are able to receive messages either at their smartphones / tablets where the mob app is installed, or at their inboxes in the public portal. The messages might concern the announcement of a new event, a planned activity, an invitation to join a community, an alert or notification about an ongoing action and so on. Members of the NGCP-SN (citizens and CP officers) are able to create reports about an incident. The reporting can take place via the Mobile App or at the public portal and might concern an incident as it evolves or users might report a past event. The reportees at any time can provide additional information or

---

[4]https://play.google.com/store/apps/details?id=com.aditess.inspect2tCitizens

clarification or even proceed with report deletion. The submitted report is directed to the police back end office where it is recorded and registered in the incidents database. The reported incident then becomes available to all backend subsystem for further processing.

Following the intake of the incident report the NGCP operator will use the back office built in intelligence to analyse the submitted reports and may share actionable information with the participants (both police officials and community members – when required). The actionable information is stored in the system. The Secure Portal operator, who is a trained police officer, based on the reported information and the recommendations of police analysts, may decide if there is need to involve CP officers/police forces from the proximate to incident locations or asked citizens to provide additional information. While an incident is being dispatched to a CP officer, the system administrator after consulting his superiors and based on the urgency of the event, they might proceed with broadcasting an alert to all users of the NGCP-SN. Police intelligence analysts and other police officials can use the INSPEC^{2}T information to publish crime factsheets in order to create critical awareness among their network members. The users should receive notification after sending or sharing/information to police.

Interaction with Other Social Networks

To expand networking the NGCP-SN members should be able to share messages with other social media networks using either the public portal or the Mobile App. The messages can originate from an INSPEC^{2}T user or a police official channel e.g. issue an Amber alert for a missing child and multicast the alert to NGCP-SN and other SM networks. The importance of interworking with existing social networks is explained with reference to recent developments[5,6] in Manchester Arena and London Bridge. The police used Twitter to channel news as they were unfolded and eliminate speculation, rumours and fake news. This highlights the need of interaction with external social networks and necessitates police vigorousness to provide regularly updates, directions and eliminate malicious reporting.

Alike existing Social Network practices, INSPEC^{2}T users should be offered the option to take part in online surveys aiming to get responses from selected groups. Police Officials can create small surveys or simple polls and release them to selected group of participants to (i) extract specific information,(ii) have them rate their security needs and (iii) asked them what type of police information is required regarding different safety issues. If the survey initiator is aiming to expand the number of respondees then the survey or polls may well be shared using third party social networking platforms.

---

[5]http://www.bbc.com/news/uk-england-manchester-40007886
[6]http://www.bbc.com/news/uk-40013040

Back End Intelligence

INSPEC[2]T is developed around a modular and open system architecture[7] which promotes interconnections with existing modules and ensures information is not lost even in the event of some modules failed to function. The NGCP operator is offered the maximum information in real-time at each stage of processing and controls the information to be published. Additionally, the operator has access to offline information, for investigating incidents "a posteriori", perform data correlation, issue reports and build expert knowledge, for future alertness and CP actions. Multimedia event data and signals are processed fast, while authenticating, classifying and ranking sources. As such the system will try to drop pseudo evidence and "decoy" attempts. The system also utilises GIS information and multimedia content. The reported incidents enriched by multimedia essence, will be processed by the INSPEC[2]T Parallel Processing modules. Analytics are applied, both to multimedia (video, images, speech) and web sources and an ontology is built and maintained.

Rules and Supporting Actions

To control possible violations and abuse within the NGCP-SN all users and administrators should follow an agreed code of conduct and terms of use. In the unlikely event that inappropriate behaviour is exercised by certain members, the affected users can alert the Community or the system Administrator and request immediate attention. Reporting of participants or community members that exercise harassment, exchange posts which contain abusive content or flag communities who use the system for other purposes for which it is not intended and indicate of inappropriate planned activities should be encouraged and promoted within a NGCP-SN. In addition, ethical, legal, societal and applicable data protection and privacy guidelines should complete the NGCP-SN terms and conditions.

INSPEC[2]T Pilot Evaluation

The first working INSPEC[2]T version undertook trials in Belfast, in April 2017. CP Officers from Police Service Northern Ireland in cooperation with fellow Officers from Lancashire Constabulary participated, along with residents from the Holyland community and members of the Ulster University in the CP scenarios execution. The second pilot and a proof of concept demo to SAG and EEG committees took

---

[7]https://pdfs.semanticscholar.org/0bde/e147a7a3f04584424f5e32a54f65299a36ea.pdf

place in Egkomi, Cyprus in May 2017. Also, in Cyprus, the consortium conducted a series of small scale pilots and solution demonstrations with engaged municipalities and LEAs. The third pilot took place in Valencia, Spain in May 2017. Further to the Valencia local police and local community involvement, there were representatives from San Sebastian Police and Guardia Civil.

NGCP Evaluation Framework

Following the development of the INSPEC^{2}T solution, an assessment framework was needed to verify whether the implemented functionalities satisfy the end user requirements. The THOR concept, which was developed by CAMINO[8] project was adapted and used for the assessment of the INSPEC^{2}T solution. The delivered solution was analysed in four dimensions as follows:

Technical Assess if the implemented solutions will assist the uptake of the NGCP-SN, and will provide the intelligence mechanisms required to analyse efficiently the user supplied information.

Human Evaluate how a series of human factors, behavioural aspects, privacy issues, ethical, societal and raising CP awareness activities will influence CP practices and more safe and secure communities.

Organisational Examine if the proposed processes, policies and procedures will enhance the cooperation between Communities and LEAs and if the project will result to better CP.

Regulatory Inspect the project for adherence to law, standards, data protection and legal framework at national and EU level.

Each one of the THOR dimensions is divided into several areas of interest based on the assessment needs identified in the previous section. Following the execution of three pilots the feedback provided and results achieved were used to identify gaps and challenges that need to be overcome. The interaction of the THOR dimensions for the identified participant/user categories for the Use Case groups is shown in Fig. 6.4.

The succeeding sections outlines how each one of the THOR dimensions constitutes a CP verification framework and how each one of the use cases are mapped under a specific dimension to provide the assessment criteria and verify whether the stakeholder requirements have been addressed and to what extent.

---

[8]http://cordis.europa.eu/project/rcn/185485_en.html

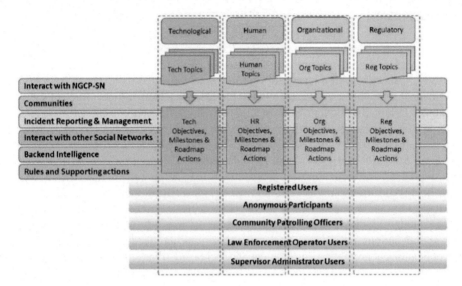

Fig. 6.4 THOR model applied to INSPEC^{2}T system

Technology

The improvements recorded by adopting technology offerings and included them in current CP practices is underlying the importance to understand which technology solutions will introduce additional value. Introducing IT to police operation is a complex and demanding task. Custers (2012) claims "it is not clear which technologies are more usable and effective in the context of a police organization". INSPEC^{2}T offers LEAs a variety of technology innovative tools like applications for mobile devices, online presence, crime and multimedia analytic software (CBR, GCEP, MMA), information sharing (Public Portal and DWH) to be explored and assessed for their impact.

Human

One of the most fundamental aspects of improving CP is to empower the communities to prevent crime or the problems that lead to it. Establishing and maintaining mutual trust is therefore the central goal of CP, as it allows wide law enforcement access to valuable community information leading potentially to the prevention and resolution of crimes (Docobo 2005). The citizens need to be aware of their own role and responsibilities and should proactively respond to indications of crime and disorder in their communities. In the INSPEC^{2}T ecosystem citizens are encourage to from and participate in communities while the project partners will assess human behaviour as a mean of collaboration, information exchange, awareness, efficacy and community building.

Organisational

The first component of successful CP initiatives involves transformational changes in the organizational structure and operation of LEAs (Bureau of Justice Assistance 1994). The organisation changes proposed were evaluated using the "Three E's" efficiency, effectiveness, and enabling. (U.S. Department of Justice, Office of Community Oriented Policing Services 2017) Briefly, *efficiency* means getting a task done with a minimum expenditure of time and effort; *effectiveness*, is doing a better job to produce an intended or expected result, and finally, technologies will *enable* LEAs to do something they could not do before. CP is an information-intensive task/process, and technology plays a central role in helping to provide ready access to quality information. Accurate and timely information makes problem-solving efforts more effective and ensures that officers are informed about the crime and community conditions of their beat (Karp and Clear 2000). Therefore, two-way communications, online reports, discussion forums, and feedback using interactive applications is promoting engagement and increasing transparency.

Regulatory

The INSPEC^{2}T system aims to combine the principles of CP with the affordances of new technologies. Both the actual and the potential utilisation of the resulting tools have to be compliant with the legal frameworks so that they can be correctly implemented in participating countries. Moreover, taking into account the effects of EU directives[9,10] and legal trends across the European Union may facilitate the exportation and application of the findings to countries that are not currently participating in the development of the INSPEC^{2}T system.[11] In order to offer a broad picture of normative debates, established regulations, other relevant documents such as agreements, recommendations and guidelines which garnered public attention and might influence future regulations or foster best practices were considered. The resulted evaluation framework used to assess the INSPEC^{2}T solution is depicted in Fig. 6.5. Following the completion of first three pilots and the execution of a small-scale pilot in the SAG and EEG workshop the consortium received end user feedback and recommendations. These in conjunction with the provided end user requirements will shape and adjust the development of the solution prior the phase-2 pilots, scheduled to take place between October and December 2017. The key outcomes of the stakeholder input are summarised hereafter.

---

[9]http://eur-lex.europa.eu/legal-content/EN/TXT/?uri=CELEX%3A32016L0680 (protection of natural persons with regard to the processing of personal data by competent authorities).

[10]http://eur-lex.europa.eu/eli/reg/2016/679/oj (protection of natural persons with regard to the processing of personal data and on the free movement of such data).

[11]D2.2 Legal and Ethical dimensions of INSPEC2T System available online at: http://inspec2t-project.eu/en/public-deliverables.

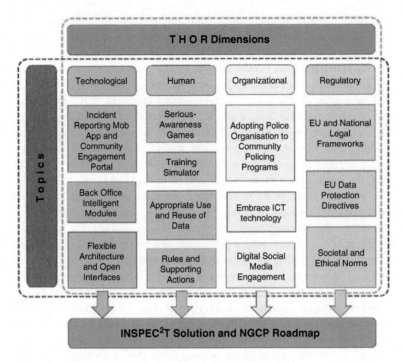

Fig. 6.5 THOR evaluation framework for INSPEC²T assessment

Interim Evaluation Findings

Using a structured questionnaire, the INSPEC²T members requested from the SAG and EEG committees to provide their feedback and guide the consortium endeavours to shape and finalise the solution to be tested in the phase-2 pilots. Consenting the incident reporting using the mobile application, 93% of the experts indicated that it is offering the greatest potential to improve CP. Similarly, 71% prompted that the application for LEAs is a great asset for CP officers in the field. For the public portal (50%) valued its use and ranked it top together with the mobile applications as a component that should be improvement to assist community building and empower citizens participation in CP tasks.

The collection of the "back office" components, (MMA, GCEP, BI, CBR, and DWH) provides the intelligence to INSPEC²T system to correlate, group and analyse the incoming reports and assists the Secure Portal operators to manage more effectively the reported incidents. The independent advisors indicated that cutting edge police command and control centers are already using a number of intelligence subsystems. Therefore, their adaptation to support CP operations is well perceived. The CAD interface supports legacy incident reporting systems; it is the gateway which feeds CP related reports that reach the call center into the INSPEC²T system and supplies the required information to its operators with the location of police resources.

All experts insisted in using open standards interfaces, as it makes sense to interconnect the demonstrated system with existing police systems like suspect databases and enhanced its functionalities. It is acknowledged that incident reporting if processes intelligently is a valuable intelligence source. Therefore, multimedia enriched content who is embedded in citizens' reports should be treated as a valuable information source. Kelling and Bratton (2006) specified that "Intelligence-led policing is crime fighting that is guided by effective intelligence gathering and analysis". Therefore, an intelligent CP system should be capable to supply and feed the existing police operational systems and if needed should have the capacity to provide facial recognition or offer acoustic event detection and alert its operators.

Lastly, the open interfaces can be utilised to forward incidents to other authorities, like the municipalities, or environmental agencies and forward reports (information) related to their scope which is reported by citizens using a CP system. After the pilot debriefing sessions with community representatives, the findings of the INSPEC^{2}T public survey,[12] where confirmed as citizens indicated that using the mobile application will result to more frequent reporting.

INSPEC^{2}T developed an awareness raising game for citizens developed for iOS and Android devices. Using a gamification approach, the citizens were encouraged to collaborate with the police for the benefit of their communities. Through this game, the citizens realised that police resources are not infinite and as such their cooperation with police in a number of incidents will result better CP results. The INSPEC^{2}T's training simulator is a scenario driven tool that simulates the submission of citizen reports and trains police operators to the functionality of the platform. The option to train CP system operators received positive feedback and it is a mandatory prerequisite for police organisations to offer customised to their needs and operational training to their CP Officers. The community and police relations in a social media like ecosystem will be studied in the phase-2 pilots. Therefore, the rules and the supporting actions required to prevent inappropriate behaviour and promote community and police interactions will be tested between October and November 2017.

The topics of EU's legal framework and data protection directives were discussed in all pilot's debriefing sessions and debated on a roundtable with SAG and EEG members. All experts agreed that the topic of data protection is well defined in EU directive 2016/680 which is designed to be consistent with the General Data Protection Regulation. Although Police officers as a competent authority, can process personal data for the "prevention of threats to public security" (Article 1), it is not clear at the moment which are the governing rules for use and reuse of data for CP purposes. The fact that the INSEPC^{2}T solution implemented adaptable safeguards for data ageing and the archiving and retention of submitted records is well perceived.

---

[12]D1.2 – "End User Requirements – 1st SAG Report" available online at: http://inspec2t-project. eu/en/public-deliverables

Likewise, the police adaptation to CP programs, the inclusion of modern ICT solutions to everyday policing tasks, and the police strategy towards digital and social media are topics outside the influenced sphere of INSPEC^{2}T or other similar initiatives. To this extent, the consortium studied and analysed a number of indicators which considered essential in implementing CP. Fostering and developing police-community relations requires active engagement from the police organisation, individual officers and community representatives. A CP maturity model is currently being developed for the purpose of producing CP policy recommendations to EU.

Conclusions

Following the completion of the first three pilots, the consortium received requests for further testing the INSPEC^{2}T solution in a variety of different CP contexts. In a number of debriefing sessions with Police officers and community members the following functionalities were valued: (1) The way of reporting incidents and contacting the police using the Mobile App. (2) Feedback about the status of submitted reports (3) Organising of information and management of incidents; (4) Reporting using multimedia content; and (5) Visualization on a map of the location of an incident. Overall incident reporting and communications via a social media network is well perceived by both Police and communities.

In sort INSPEC^{2}T was considered a substantial transition in the way of working for both the police and the citizen and to their mutual relationship, while Police officers were positive about the technical capabilities of the solution. The consortium members are currently working to incorporate the provided suggestion into the platform, evolve existing features and add new functionalities prior to the second testing phase. The final system tests will take place in Groningen (the Netherlands) between September and December 2017 (for 9 weeks) and in Preston (England) in November 2017.

Acknowledgment The work presented in this paper received funding from the European Commission, under the "H2020-FCT-2014 Ethical/Societal Dimension Topic 2: Enhancing cooperation between law enforcement agencies and citizens – Community policing" call entitled INSPEC^{2}T (Inspiring CitizeNS Participation for Enhanced Community PoliCing AcTions) under grant agreement number 653749.

References

Bureau of Justice Assistance. (1994). *Understanding community policing, a framework for action.* Washington, DC: U.S. Department of Justice.
Custers, B. (2012). Technology in policing: Experiences, obstacles and police needs. *Computer Law & Security Review, 28,* 62–68.

Docobo, J. (2005). Community Policing as the Primary Prevention Strategy for Homeland Security at the Local Law Enforcement Level. *Homeland Security Affairs, 1*, Article 4.

Gans, H. (1982). *The urban villagers: Group and class in the life of Italian-Americans*. New York: Free Press (Macmillan Co., Inc.).

Johnston, L. (2005). From 'community' to 'neighbourhood' policing: Police community support officers and the 'police extended family' in London. *Journal of Community & Applied Social Psychology, 15*, 241–254.

Karp, D., & Clear, T. (2000). Community justice – A conceptual framework. *Criminal Justice, 2*, 323–368.

Kelling, G., & Bratton, W. (2006). *Policing terrorism, civic bulletin 43*. New York: Manhattan Institute for Policy Research.

Kenney, D., & McNamara, R. (1999). *Police and policing: Contemporary issues*. London: Greenwood Publishing Group.

Manning, P. K. (2011). *Crime mapping, information technology, and the rationality of crime control*. NYU Press.

Peak, K. (2013). *Encyclopedia of community policing and problem solving*. University of Nevada, Reno: SAGE Publications.

Tilley, N. (2008). Modern approaches to policing: Community, problem-oriented and intelligence-led. In *Handbook of policing*. Routledge Handbooks Online.

Trottier, D. (2015). Open source intelligence, social media and law enforcement: Visions, constraints and critiques. *European Journal of Cultural Studies, 18*, 530–547.

U.S. Department of Justice, Office of Community Oriented Policing Services. (2017). [Online]. Available at: https://ric-zai-inc.com/Publications/cops-p157-pub.pdf

Whyte, W. (1943). *Street corner society: The social structure of an Italian slum*. Chicago: Chicago University Press.

Chapter 7
Next Generation of CP: The Unity IT Toolkit

Clara Ayora and Natasha Newton

Introduction

Traditionally, community policing (CP) constitutes an important tool for Law Enforcement Agencies (LEAs). Communities of people, despite their varying social, cultural, geographic, and ethnic differences, have common and shared values in their need for safety, security and wellbeing. Under the CP philosophy, LEAs are empowered to identify and solve problems proactively and jointly within their communities (Unity – *Document of Work* 2015).

However, despite the current technical connectivity, many citizens and their communities are disengaged from LEAs and other key stakeholders, which has a detrimental effect on CP. Coupling new technologies with traditional CP activities, for example foot patrol, leaflets, and local events, provides a means to further strengthen the cooperation between LEAs, Stakeholders, and Citizens. In this context, the Unity project was proposed. Its fundamental vision is to strengthen the connection between the LEAs and communities to maximize the safety and security of all citizens (Unity Deliverable 3.1 2015). This is achieved through a series of interlocking primary objectives:

- To capture best practices for cooperation between police and citizens;
- To design, develop and deliver training for LEAs and awareness raising activities about CP;

C. Ayora (✉)
Treelogic. S.L., Madrid, Spain
e-mail: clara.aora@treelogic.com

N. Newton
Rinicom Ltd, Lancaster, UK
e-mail: natasha@rinicom.com

© The Author(s) 2018
G. Leventakis, M. R. Haberfeld (eds.), *Community-Oriented Policing and Technological Innovations*, SpringerBriefs in Criminology,
https://doi.org/10.1007/978-3-319-89294-8_7

- To develop a communications technology to facilitate, strengthen and accelerate the communication between citizens and police.

This chapter describes the technology used in Unity as a facilitator of CP against the 6 key pillars identified during the UNITY project; (1) trust and confidence building, (2) accountability, (3) information sharing and communication, (4) addressing local needs, (5) collaboration, and (6) crime prevention (Unity Deliverable 7.3 2016). The *Unity IT Toolkit* (herein 'ToolKit') is a suite of features that cover the best practices used to support and assist CP methods across all stakeholders (e.g., forums, news, events, instant messages, posting documents, social media and calendars, among others). These features work in tandem to provide an effective CP ToolKit. In addition, it is based on a number of modular design principles that support the flexibility, stability and robustness of the ToolKit, whilst ensuring security standards are complied with.

Given the variable casuistry of the different countries, the ToolKit needs to be instantiated for addressing each specific community (and therefore their specific needs and contexts). In particular, the ToolKit is parameterized and customized for eight live pilots within Croatia (month 6 of the project), Estonia (M11), Germany (M17), Belgium (M21), Finland (M26), Bulgaria (M29), Macedonia (M30) and the UK (M30). Their major goal is to test and validate with end users (i.e., LEAs, relevant stakeholders, and citizens) that CP could be enhanced by using the ToolKit, best practice processes and training. For each pilot, the ToolKit is adapted to the community's requirements adding or removing features as needed. In addition, to facilitate the mobility, the ToolKit is also implemented as a mobile app, taking advantage of the rich number of features that smart phones provide (e.g., bi-directional communication capabilities with the communities).

Unity IT Toolkit Architecture

The architectural design of the ToolKit ensures that a modular, flexible, extensible, scalable, robust and secure system is produced. The design process focused on facilitating the 6 pillars of CP using the technology as an enabler. This allowed for a trust-based, cooperative CP to be delivered in an efficient and effective way between LEA's, stakeholders and citizens. In addition, the bi-directional communication capabilities offered by mobile application technologies, combined with advanced data analytics enhances the LEA officers ability to make strategic decisions. The provision of 'other applications' (3rd party) has also been addressed and refers to integration with third party applications, this covers any application outside of the ToolKit which may interact by pushing/pulling information from it.

The architectural design places a strong emphasis on the user interface guidelines, which by default addresses the security analysis, by presenting a full threat model that uses the attacker's point of view to identify a list of threats that could undermine the trustworthiness of the system.

The implementation of the Web Portal and Mobile Application (herein 'app') of the ToolKit takes into account the various views of the system, including; functional, data, business pro-cess, deployment, accessibility, usability, security, internationalisation/ localisation, resilience, performance and scalability. For the purpose of this chapter, focus will be placed on the functionality and usability of the web portal and app. The latter acts as a small screen wrapper of sorts, replicating the functions and features of the web portal, utilising the same functionalities, API calls and dependencies as its larger screened counterpart. Therefore, it is not necessary to duplicate the same functional view.

The Usability perspective addresses all aspects related to the User Interface of the ToolKit. The components that expose a User Interface include three main areas:

1. The header bar and footer areas – these areas are always displayed to the user on all pages. They include elements that may be of use to the user at any time. However, the actual contents in the header/ footer bars may change, depending on the user role.
2. The navigation menu – like the header bar, this area is always visible to the user on all pages. It allows the user to quickly navigate to the core pages of the portal, from anywhere in the portal. Again, as for the header bar, the options available in the navigation menu depend on the role of the user;
3. The contents area – this area is where the portal contents are presented. It is highly dynamic as it displays the contents of each web page. The user may vertically scroll through the displayed contents in this area.

The iOS and Android apps capture the primary functionalities of the portal itself, but with appropriate design, user interface and user experience considerations made to accommodate the unique functionalities, and in some cases limitations, of touch screen mobile devices.

The primary means of navigation within the app utilises a 'pull out' style map – replicating the same basic layout of the web platform's navigation menu. As with the portal, the options provided to the user depends on their level of authentication within the system; anonymous, registered citizen, registered LEA/Stakeholder or Administrator. For the mobile implementation of the menu, a user can select from the pull-out list to open the precise area of the app they wish to view or use. The organisation of functionality and options within the app closely mirrors that of the web portal. The user can clearly see from the home-screen their respective levels of access within the app.

The use of cookies is a typical technique to improve the usability of the system for the users. However, in cases where this technique is used, when a user accesses the web portal for the first time a disclaimer is presented stating that the cookie policy is in use. If the user does not agree with the cookie policy, the cookies cannot be used. If the user agrees with the cookie policy, the disclaimer will not be displayed again.

The contents accessible via the web portal depend on two aspects:

- The role of the user – different roles can access different functionality. This impacts the available options in the navigation bar, the information presented in the header and the web page contents;
- The selected community –users select their community of interest – usually a geographical local area but may be a virtual community too – and the web portal should only display contents that are relevant to the selected community.

The aim of the data driven analytics engine is to assist LEAs and other relevant stakeholders and stakeholders to explore and understand the issues and concerns underpinning the amount of information managed by Unity. Several technologies are involved to choreograph the functionality of the engine (e.g., MongoDB for the database, Python for implementing the features, Apache Tomcat for the web application). The engine supports the following features:

- A tag cloud: To identify topics, entities, organizations or locations in the ToolKit forum (e.g., what are people talking about in a thread). The importance of each tag is shown with different sizes and colours. The more relevant the term is, the bigger it appears;
- A sentiment analysis: To identify whether public opinion is evolving positively or negatively on a given subject
- A relationship graph: To identify cross relations among the tags of the tag cloud (e.g., two topics appear always together);
- External and public data mining: To identify similar interests between the users of the Toolkit and other external communities (e.g., Twitter or Facebook).

This engine is not conceived as an intelligence tool, instead it improves information sharing between LEAs and the communities in a transparent way as well as trust building by dealing with mid-term and long-term community-related problems.

Finally, the CP Strategy Generator (CPSG) is an intuitive tool developed with the purpose of achieving the following objectives:

- Accumulate and present all Unity research, analysis, and technology;
- Collect Current and Target operating information during each pilot and to provide a data repository for CP across Europe;
- Planning of CP strategy by LEA's

The CPSG is based loosely on strategic CP in the UK, encouraging users to look at their internal strategies in relation to Strategic, Tactical, and Operational improvements. The CPAG (Community Policing Architecture Glossary) framework is used to denote the potential capability areas users would look to improve with the CPSG, and from this, the Current and Target Operating Models are generated.

The CPSG takes on an iterative and inclusive approach, encouraging users to input any gaps in the data through their own experiences. The outcome is an auto-generated PDF report which users can review against their current strategies to determine any areas of improvement and enables data to be shared throughout Europe.

End User Assessment

Given the variable casuistry of the different countries, the ToolKit is instantiated for addressing each specific community need and context. In particular, the ToolKit has been parameterized and customized for eight live pilots during the whole project. After each pilot, key focus groups were held with end users to understand perceived benefits after using an instantiation of the ToolKit.

The overall consensus was positive, end users advised they can see the real potential the ToolKit could have in real life scenarios, however due to the limited timeframes available for the pilots they were unable to test this theory effectively. In several cases direct comparisons to existing platforms were highlighted, including Facebook, Twitter, WhatsApp and Doodle poll. Unity is working towards integrating with exiting platforms where possible as it understands the potential barrier to adopting new technology, especially in older generations. That being said, with prior training and user manuals the user experience of the ToolKit could also be enhanced through a shared understanding of the benefits Unity provides.

As with all technology, there was a concern across all pilots regarding the possibility of end users misusing the ToolKit for criminal behaviour or as another way to report emergencies. All efforts have been taken to mitigate this risk by including disclaimers clearly highlighting the tool does not replace existing emergency channels, and that all communication will be monitored by LEA's.

Future pilots will seek input from citizens to review the marketability and trust within a community to use the proposed ToolKit. This places emphasis on the proper exploitation of the tool, ensuring end users buy-in to the concept and understand the real value of such a system. To achieve this, the LEA's within the consortium will liaise closely with their respective communities, providing them with the necessary training and support required.

Conclusions

The Unity IT ToolKit has been defined in the context of the Unity project that is intended to strengthen the connection between the LEAs and their communities to maximize the safety and security of all citizens. Through different views and perspectives, a set of features are implemented including forums, news, events, instant messages, posting documents, social media and calendars, among others. In addition, a data driven analytics engine has been included to support decision-making for all the different stakeholders to cooperatively plan actuations for improvement. Finally, the CP Strategy Generator is an intuitive tool to collect operating information, to provide a data repository for CP, and to plan CP strategy by LEA's.

To facilitate its adoption, the ToolKit has been implemented as a desktop application and as a mobile application, both in iOS and Android. All the implemented features are parameterized and customized for eight live pilots, for which the major goal is to test and validate with end users that CP could be enhanced by using the ToolKit, best practice processes and training.

During key focus groups, end users envisioned the real potential of the ToolKit, identifying particular scenarios it would be beneficial. However, due to the limited timeframes available for trialling the ToolKit, users were unable to test this theory effectively. Also, they directly compare it to existing platforms such as WhatsApp. We consider that with prior training and user manuals, the user experience could be enhanced through a shared understanding of the Unity's benefits.

Going forwards, during the project, future instantiations of the ToolKit will be re-evaluated by end users to gather a further understanding of the impact it could have on CP from a marketability and trust perspective. A detailed exploitation plan will be drafted as prat of the project, clearly identifying the route to commercialisation and it is expected the end user partners within the consortium will be the initial early adopters of the ToolKit post-project.

References

Unity – *Document of Work*. (2015). Grant Agreement No: 653729 – Horizon 2020. European Union.
Unity Deliverable 3.1. (2015). *Report on existing approaches and best/effective practices to community policing*. European Union Horizon 2020 Programme under grant agreement no 653729.
Unity Deliverable 7.3. (2016). *Report on results of the baseline measurements*. European Union Horizon 2020 Programme under grant agreement no 653729.

Chapter 8
A Descriptive, Practical, Hybrid Argumentation Model to Assist with the Formulation of Defensible Assessments in Uncertain Sense-Making Environments

Celeste Groenewald, Simon Attfield, Peter Passmore, B. L. William Wong, and Neesha Kodagoda

Introduction

Criminal Intelligence Analysis has been described as, "a philosophy which sets out how we can approach the investigation of crime and criminals by using the intelligence and information that we have collected concerning them. It provides techniques that structure our natural deductive powers and thought processes, the 'natural intuition', which proficient investigators use subconsciously all the time. It also provides tools that help us to understand the information we collect, and to communicate that understanding to others" (UNODC 2011).

The Authorised Professional Practice (APP) states that intelligence is, "collected information that has been developed for action" and that it may be classified as "sensitive or confidential" (HMIC 2015). The reliability of information, as intelligence, is recorded and managed through the 5 x 5 x 5 model (College of Policing 2016).

The United Nations Office on Drugs and Crime's (UNODC) description also outlines the inference making aspect of Criminal Intelligence Analysis and the need for techniques to assist with the structuring of these often tacit processes. The National Intelligence Model (NIM) stipulates the aim of crime analysis as, "to interpret a range of information to develop inferences, which are conclusions about what is known or what is believed to be happening" (CENTREX 2007). The purpose of these techniques is to increase understanding surrounding the 5WH questions (who, what, when, where and how) and to predict harm, threats, risks and opportunities.

C. Groenewald (✉) · S. Attfield · P. Passmore · B. L. William Wong · N. Kodagoda
Middlesex University, London, UK
e-mail: c.groenewald@mdx.ac.uk; s.attfield@mdx.ac.uk; p.passmore@mdx.ac.uk;
w.wong@mdx.ac.uk; n.kodagoda@mdx.ac.uk

© The Author(s) 2018
G. Leventakis, M. R. Haberfeld (eds.), *Community-Oriented Policing and Technological Innovations*, SpringerBriefs in Criminology,
https://doi.org/10.1007/978-3-319-89294-8_8

The final part of UNODC's description regarding criminal intelligence analysis outlines the need for tools to assist with the collection, comprehension and dissemination of intelligence between members of law enforcement organisations. Examples of these tool are: association and network charts; timelines and sequence of events charts; comparative case charts; maps, flow charts; frequency charts; story boards and mind maps. Maps, graphs and tables mainly assist with Crime Pattern Analysis (CPA) whereas flow charts tend to assist with Crime Business Analysis (CBA) (College of Policing 2016).

The next section describes the method used to conduct our relevant studies. This is followed with an outline of the main literature and results describing the proposed practical hybrid argumentation model.

Method

In order to construct our initial, descriptive, practical, hybrid argumentation model (see Fig. 8.1), we have conducted separate studies in order to obtain our results and they are outlined below (refer to the colour coding to see the contribution of each study to our model).

- Study A (Purple Coding): Interview with an experienced Operational Intelligence Analyst from West Midlands Police, UK (Groenewald and Attfield 2016, unpublished)
- Study B (Green Coding): Think-Steps: A Field Study with four Criminal Intelligence Analysts (Selvaraj et al. 2016).
- Study C (Yellow Coding): Sense-making Triangle: Multiple qualitative studies to determine how criminal intelligence analysts think. (Wong 2014; Wong and Kodagoda 2016; Gerber et al. 2016)
- Study D & E (Blue & Pink Coding): Sense-Making Issues & Managing Significance: Qualitative Studies of eleven cognitive task analysis interviews with five experienced operational intelligence analysts (Groenewald et al. 2017a, b)
- The white areas are covered by the literature.

Each publication outlines the relevant methodology in detail. Here we provide an overview of the studies.

The qualitative studies (Study C, D and E) analysed the transcripts from Cognitive Task Analysis (CTA) interviews with five experienced Operational Criminal Intelligence Analysts. The interviewers, using the Critical Decision Method (CDM) (Klein et al. 1986), investigated the inference and sense making processes of the Operational Criminal Intelligence Analyst participants from different police forces in the UK and Belgium. A third-party anonymised, transcribed and reviewed the transcripts due to the sensitivity of the contents it contained. Different researchers independently performed data analysis using the same set of transcripts.

Study A was an interview with an Operational Intelligence Analyst from West Midlands Police (UK) to understand the use of the 'Day Book'. The Day Book is a means by which analysts record their daily activities and tasks related to an investigation. The interview lasted 40 min and used open-ended questions to gather the information from the analyst.

Selvaraj et al. (2016) conducted a field study (Study B) with four experienced Criminal Intelligence Analysts at the European Federal Police station. They conducted one-to-one interviews with each officer which lasted four and a half hours each.

Literature Review and Results

Results from each study are outlined below along with the relevant literature related to each section. The colour coding highlights the sections covered within our initial, descriptive, practical, hybrid argumentation model (Fig. 8.1).

Schemas (Green Coding)

Passmore et al. (2015) described the importance and functionality of different types of evidential structuring and reasoning approaches, as found within a wide set of literature dedicated to the research of uncertain sense-making environments. The evidential structuring and reasoning approaches described by Passmore et al. (2015) encompassed **argumentation schemas** (Wigmore 1931; Wagenaar et al.

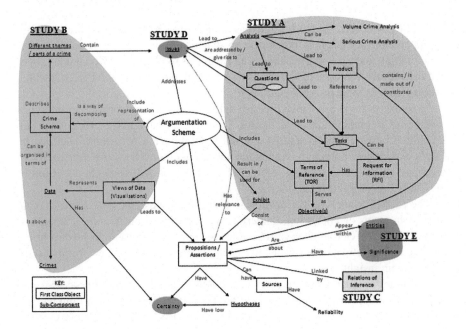

Fig. 8.1 Our initial, descriptive, practical, hybrid argumentation model with research colour codings

1993; Toulmin 2003; Bex et al. 2006; Allen et al. 2015), **narrative** (Pennington and Hastie 1992; Rao 2003; Bruner 2004; Segel and Heer 2010; Attfield and Blandford 2011; Chapin et al. 2013) and **thematic sorting** (Pirolli and Card 2005; Attfield and Blandford 2011; Rooney et al. 2014) and the role that each served during sense-making and analytical activities. Passmore et al. (2015) urged that any software application design that is aimed at supporting thinking and reasoning throughout analytical and problem-solving tasks, should incorporate a hybrid of structuring and reasoning approaches.

Bex and Verheij (2013) described factual story schemas as "determining which accounts of facts are plausible and which gaps need to be filled by further evidence to form a full picture of what happened". It need not only be true for facts, but can also encapsulate assertions or propositions made by the user.

Selvaraj et al. (2016) conducted research in understanding crime schematisation within Criminal Intelligence Analysis and proposed the concept of "Think Steps". "Think Steps" have been defined by Selvaraj et al. (2016) as "providing a template that allows the analyst to approach the case, decompose it into separate elements and classify associated data accordingly". Although Klein et al. (2007) defined the use of frames (as schematisation) in their Data Frame Model, Selvaraj et al. (2016) have tailored their work specifically for the Criminal Intelligence Analysis domain, thus allowing for greater understanding on how analysts work.

Relations of Inference (Yellow Coding)

Before any evidential structuring and reasoning approach can be incorporated within an application design, it is imperative to understand how the users in the target domain think and reason. This has been researched by Wong and Kodagoda (2016) and their results can been expressed as a sense-making triangle (see Fig. 8.2) which encompasses of three interlinked triangles.

The inner triangle is the inference-triangle and describes the process of inference making as a combination of deductive, inductive and abductive processes. Each inferential process type is interlinked and a combination of factors, such as the user's experience, domain and situation knowledge as well as the availability of information, determines which inferential process type will be at the forefront of the user's thinking and reasoning.

The second triangle is the anchoring-triangle and describes the sense-making process in terms of anchoring, laddering and associative questioning (Wong and Kodagoda 2016). Gerber et al. (2016) added the third insight-triangle, by describing the role that intuition and leap-of-faith plays, in highly uncertain environments, in order to gain insight.

All three triangles work together in a complex combination of processes and sequences and forms an integral part of the tacit processes of human thinking and reasoning. The work of Wong (2014) and Wong and Kodagoda (2016) relies greatly on the foundational research of Klein et al. (2007) and Kahneman (2011) on the human thinking processes.

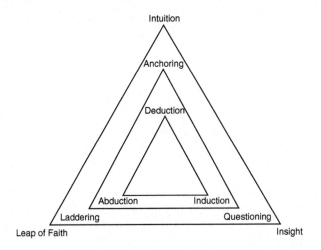

Fig. 8.2 Depiction of Wong and Kodagoda's (2016) sense-making triangle

Kahneman (2011) introduced the concepts of System 1 and System 2 thinking. System 1 thinking is related to quick instinctive thinking, based on what a person is presented with. System 2 thinking is a more deliberate and slow type of thinking, predominantly used in difficult problem-solving tasks.

Klein et al. (2007) described the thinking process in terms of their Data Frame Theory (DFT). DFT makes use of the concept of frames, where a frame represents the initial understanding a person has about a particular situation. When the situation is unfamiliar, the frame will be weak as there is no prior knowledge or experience to guide action. A person can elaborate the frame by searching for related information, thus adding to and expanding the frame. The selection process of information to add to the frame can undergo a questioning process. When contradictory information is found, then the frame is compared to other frames in order to determine the most viable option.

Macro-Cognition (Blue, Pink and Purple Coding)

Prior to this, Klein and Klinger (1991) researched how people make decisions in natural settings where time constraints inhibited them from using deliberate analytical methods such as Multi-Attribute Utility Analysis (MAUA) and Decision Analysis. Decisions in these situations where based on prior experiences to "meet the needs of the situation" and to "recognise and classify a situation" (Klein and Klinger 1991). This hinted towards the use of System 1 thinking where there was no time for the utilisation of System 2 thinking. Klein and Klinger (1991) produced a macro-cognition model which explained that there are a multitude of factors which influenced decision making within a natural setting as appose to a controlled laboratory setting. Designing interfaces with a macro-cognitive view in mind, should cover a wider variety of influential factors, thus create a more 'complete' and natural user interface.

Hammond et al. (1987) argued on the premise that "both cognitive processes and task conditions can be arranged on a continuum that ranges from intuition to analysis". If this is true, then a macro-cognitive approach would incorporate an extensive area on the continuum, both in terms of cognitive processes and the task conditions in which a user would find themselves in. It would also mean that Kahneman's (2011) System 1 and System 2 thinking would be spread across the continuum along with the properties of Wong and Kodagoda (2016) and Gerber et al.'s (2016) sense-making triangle.

We do not wish to dispute the cognitive properties as defined by the mentioned authors, but we would like to know what would be required for a user to be aware of and to be able to defend their choices, as assessments, as they move along the continuum of intuition to analysis.

The macro-cognitive model of Klein et al. (2003) outlines the supporting macro-cognitive processes as: maintaining common ground; developing mental models; turning leverage points into courses of management; uncertainty management; attention management; mental stimulation and storyboarding. The processes of 'developing mental models' and 'mental stimulation and storyboarding' are covered by the research of the authors in the 'schemas' and 'relations to inferencing' sections outlined above. The remainder of the supporting macro-cognitive processes are outlined below.

Uncertainty Management (Blue Coding) 'Uncertainty management' within Criminal Intelligence Analysis has been researched by Groenewald et al. (2017a) and they outlined various problems (or issues) that an analyst could encounter as part of a crime schema and the properties of uncertainty that accompanied each. Each issue adds to the uncertainty in relation to analysts' thinking and reasoning efforts. Issues can crop up during any phase of the analysis, thus casting a long lasting shadow of uncertainty onto the analyst's mind. Analysts have thus developed expert strategies to work their way through each type of uncertainty (skeptisism, suspiciousness, complexity, obscurity, disparity, gaps, misconceptions, exhausted options; errors (data quality) and mental blocks) as it surfaces during analytical activities.

Attention Management (Blue Coding) Klein et al. (2003) outlined the requirement for 'attention management' as a supportive process within their macro-cognition model. Moore and Dunham (1995) refers to attention management within coordinated activities as, "when team members help each other direct their attention to signals, activities and changes that are important" (in Klein et al. 2005). As our analysts work mostly independently, the system should take on the role as a team member and assist with attention management. Groenewald et al. (2017b) concentrated on how analysts observe significant information and categorised it under attention management, because the analyst is required to decide which information is important and worthy of their attention at different stages of the analysis process.

Groenewald et al. (2017b) identified three examples on how analysts observe and extract significant information and those instances were during situations where the most certain information about an entity was known, or where the analyst deemed the information to be interesting or strange. An entity refers to an object or a person that appears in the information. The examples provided by Groenewald et al. (2017b) illustrated how analysts turned their observations into actionable items.

Maintaining Common Ground (Pink and Purple Coding) Klein et al. (2005) explained common ground refers to, "the pertinent mutual knowledge, mutual beliefs and mutual assumptions that support interdependent actions in some joint activity." The analysts we interviewed were mostly single operators working individually on sense-making tasks. We did however consider that they might have a need to manage significant information during the sense-making task. This could loosely be considered as a type of common ground between the analyst, their thoughts and the outputs from the various systems they use, as the analyst needs to keep track of their many different findings and attempts to solve the sense-making problem they are presented with.

Two separate studies have been conducted. The first covered the management of significant information and is described by Groenewald et al. (2017b) as a lifecycle consisting out of cataloguing, comparing and tracking activities. The second study was by means of an interview with an experience criminal intelligence analyst from West Midlands Police regarding the purpose of the Day Book (Groenewald and Attfield, unpublished).

STUDY 1 If Klein et al.'s (2007) frames are considered to represent the mental representation of an analyst's understanding, then entities can be considered as the externalisation of a mental frame. The thinking and inference activities of an analyst can be described in terms of Klein et al.'s (2007) creation, elaboration, questioning and reframing processes. With the assistance of lifecycles, each of Klein et al.'s (2007) cognitive processes can be matched with physical application processes, such as cataloguing, comparing and tracking activities. The cognitive processes are explained by Wong and Kodagoda (2016) and Gerber et al.'s (2016) Sense-Making triangle. The externalisation of these processes by means of entities and their lifecycles could aid the Sense-Making triangle from an interactive-design perspective.

By externalising the cognitive processes, could assist with the assessment of exhibits produced by analysts for input into decision making for Intelligence-Led Policing or evidence in a court of law.

STUDY 2 The Day Book (Groenewald and Attfield, unpublished) is a means by which analysts record their daily activities and tasks related to an investigation. The analyst also reported making use of a Blue Book which resembles a 'business diary' or a 'to-do' list. All notes related to the case are admissible, regardless of which book it is written in. Separate books make it quicker and easier for analysts to hand one book to a disclosure officer, rather than having to go through multiple books in order to remove non-case-specific information.

The process in which the Day Book plays a part is as follow: (1) The analyst is briefed by the Investigative Officer on what is required of them. This can take place in a briefing room or a one-to-one discussion. The briefing serves as the (2) Terms of Reference which the analyst would note down in their Day Book along with general information such as contact numbers. The analyst would then divide the request into one or more (3) Main Tasks which might be sub-divided into different (4) Sub-Tasks. This is noted in the Day Book with the required justification on why the analyst is performing these tasks. This is an ongoing process and expands as the analysis progresses. The (5) Results of each sub/task are briefly described. The results can serve as (6) Products or Intelligence which can later on be used as (7) Exhibits for court. The analyst may (8) Request further information from the Investigative Officer based on the Products/Intelligence produced. Likewise, the Investigative Officer may make subsequent requests to the Analyst which may be in the form of an email. The analyst does not normally produce reports, but they will produce a (9) Statement at the end of their analysis, describing what they have done and why, alongside the required supporting Exhibits.

The Day Book is a useful tool for analysts which serve to log tasks, subtasks, their outcomes and the relevant exhibits produced. It is also more than just a logging facility – it serves as a way to orient themselves in the analysis in order to remind them of what they have done and why. It also aids as a decision-support tool, so that they can understand what have influenced their decisions and how to proceed when they get stuck or run out of options.

This concludes the results of each study as well as the supporting literature. The next section discusses the initial, descriptive, practical, hybrid argumentation model that we constructed using the results from the various studies.

Discussion and Conclusion

Our aim was to construct an initial, descriptive, practical, hybrid argumentation model which should assist end-users (as criminal intelligence analysts) with the formulation of assessments in uncertain sense-making environments. We wanted to create an argumentation model that describes the different activities spanning both cognitive and physical, thus making this a hybrid model.

The main reason for deviating from the established literature on argumentation formulation, such as described by Bex et al. (2006), is that the established research supports a very rigorous approach to evidential reasoning and may not support our end-users sufficiently with the creation of defensible assessments, in environments that are influenced by high uncertainty, constant change and lack of supporting information.

We have therefore conducted numerous studies, as outlined in the previous sections, to understand how end-users in these uncertain sense-making environments make inferences, create mental models of observations and how they externalise these unconscious processes. By combining the results of our various studies, we were able to construct an initial, descriptive, practical, hybrid, argumentation model that outlines the first order concepts and their sub-components that we deemed as significant (See Fig. 8.3).

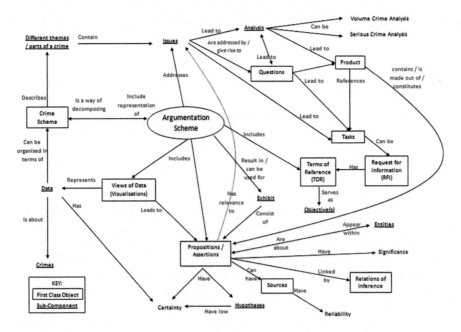

Fig. 8.3 Initial practical hybrid argumentation model

Our initial, descriptive, practical, hybrid argumentation model includes views of different data (visualisations) which represents data. The user's observations from the visualisations leads to numerous propositions/assertions (Selvaraj et al. 2016; Wong and Kodagoda 2016). In our research, the data has (or is) about different crimes. As seen with our research on schematisation (Selvaraj et al. 2016) data can be organised in terms of crime schemas, which is a useful tool for describing different themes or different parts of a crime. An argumentation scheme is therefore a way of decomposing (such as with think-steps) an argumentation scheme into manageable pieces. We therefore recommend that an argumentation scheme should include one or more representations of crime schemas to be effective within the user's environment. As the user works through different parts (or themes) of a crime, he/she will undoubtedly run into various issues (or sense-making problems), which suggests that an argumentation scheme should assist with addressing these issues as and when they are encountered. (Groenewald et al. 2017a) have outlined various types of issues (or sense-making problems) that users encounter and the various strategies they used to navigate their way through them. Issues therefore leads to analysis which can either be in the form of volume crime analysis or serious crime analysis.

Depending on the analysis style of the end-user, issues can lead to a question-based or a task-based approach. With a question-based approach the end-user prefers to address issues by asking various questions (Selvaraj et al. 2016; Wong and Kodagoda 2016) and then to perform tasks that would provide answers to those questions. The answers leads to the creation of products that consist, is made out of or constitutes various propositions or assertions. With a task-based approach

(Groenewald and Attfield, unpublished) the end-user prefers to divide the issue into manageable tasks that can be tracked and various questions could be considered whilst the task is being performed. The outcomes of a task leads to the creation of products. With a task-based approach, the end-user would reference each product with a task number in order to assist with back-tracking their activities. Some tasks are purely based on requests for information which is limited to the scope of the terms of reference. The terms of reference therefore serves as an analytical objective for the user and ensures that the user does not go off topic. The argumentation scheme should therefore include the terms of reference to make the scope of the analytical activities transparent and to ensure that all activities are relevant to the objective.

As the products contain numerous propositions and assertions from the end-user, the argumentation scheme should include propositions/assertions, which subsequently has relevance to various issues. Each proposition/assertion has a level of certainty tied to it (Groenewald et al. 2017a). When propositions/assertions are expressed as a hypothesis, then the certainty is low. Each proposition/assertion has a level of significance tied to it and each can be about a specific entity (Groenewald et al. 2017b). Propositions/assertions can have different sources and each source can have a level of significance, which are usually expressed and managed by the 5 x 5 x 5 model (College of Policing 2016). Propositions/assertions are linked by relations of inference (Wong and Kodagoda 2016; Gerber et al. 2016) which governs the entire thinking and reasoning process.

Once all the objectives, as stipulated by the terms of reference, have been met – the argumentation scheme can result in (or be used for) the creation of exhibits, which is a summary of all the propositions/assertions made by the user. Exhibits are used as input for the decision making process in Intelligence-Led policing as well as serving as evidence in a court of law.

It is our hope that our initial, descriptive, practical argumentation model could form the basis of further research with the aim of affording software developers with an understanding of the variety of sense-making activities that should be supported. Alongside this, it should also provide clues on how to design interactive interfaces that support the thinking and reasoning activities of end-users, which are embedded within the sense-making activities.

The next phase of this research is to test the feasibility of our initial, descriptive, practical argumentation model in an uncertain sense-making environment. Our user-base consists out of numerous experienced criminal intelligence analysts from West-Midlands Police (UK) as well as the Belgium police. This is fortunate for us, as we will have access to end-users that are accustomed to solve many different types of sense-making problems, using many different types of processes and procedures.

The initial design of the low fidelity user interface is depicted in Fig. 8.4. The low fidelity prototype implements the different argumentation concepts of our model. Our low fidelity prototype will consist out of grouped text boxes in a word document to simulate web-based widgets. By using a low fidelity prototype, we hope that our end-users will change the designs to fit their needs. This should allow us to test the applicability of the concepts and get a sense of how the end-users would

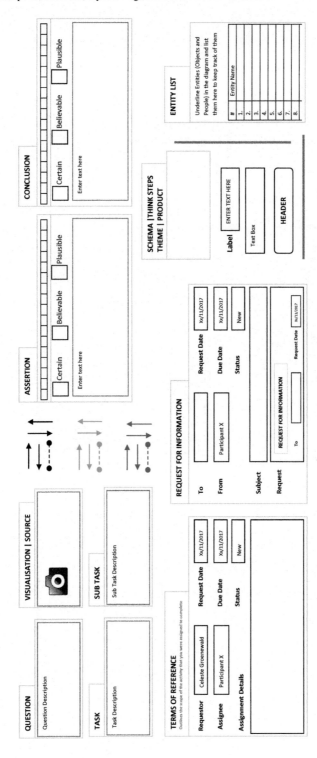

Fig. 8.4 Low fidelity user interface design, representing our initial, descriptive, practical, hybrid argumentation concepts

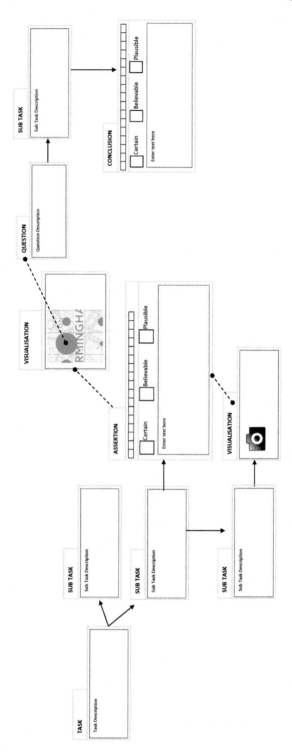

Fig. 8.5 Example of linking the initial, descriptive, practical, hybrid argumentation concepts together

prefer the look-and-feel of each 'widget'. Figure 8.5 depicts an example on how the argumentation map could be constructed by the end-users. The study will commence mid November 2017 with our end-users from West Midlands Police and the Belgium Police.

Acknowledgements The research results reported here has received funding from the European Union Seventh Framework Programme (FP7/2007-2013) through Project VALCRI, European Commission Grant Agreement N° FP7-IP-608142, awarded to B.L. William Wong, Middlesex University and partners. We are also very grateful for the enthusiasm of the police analysts in sharing with us their experiences that made this report possible.

References

Allen, C., Taylor, C., & Nairns, J. (2015). *Practical guide to evidence*. Oxford: Routledge.

Attfield, S., & Blandford, A. (2011). Making sense of digital footprints in team-based legal investigations: The acquisition of focus. *Human–Computer Interaction, 26*(1–2), 38–71.

Bex, F., & Verheij, B. (2013). Legal stories and the process of proof. *Artificial Intelligence and Law, 21*(3), 253–278.

Bex, F., Prakken, H., & Verhey, B. (2006). Anchored narratives in reasoning about evidence. *Jurix, 152*, 11–20. Available at: http://www.florisbex.com/papers/Jurix2006.pdf

Bruner, J. (2004). *Making stories: Law, literature, Life*. Harvard University Press. ISBN-13: 978–0674010994.

CENTREX. (2007). *Centrex practice advice: Introduction to intelligence-led policing*. Available at: http://www.fairplayforchildren.org/pdf/1291430265.pdf

Chapin, L., Attfield, S., & Okoro, E. M. (2013). Predictive coding, storytelling and god: Narrative understanding in e-discovery. *British Journal of Industrial Relations*.

College of Policing. (2016). *College of policing – Research and analysis*. Available at: https://www.app.college.police.uk/app-content/intelligence-management/analysis/

Gerber, M., Wong, B. W., & Kodagoda, N. (2016, September). How analysts think: Intuition, leap of faith and insight. In *Proceedings of the Human Factors and Ergonomics Society Annual Meeting* (Vol. 60, No. 1, pp. 173–177). Sage/Los Angeles: SAGE Publications.

Groenewald, C., & Attfield, S. (2016). *Interview with an experienced operational intelligence analyst from West Midlands Police, UK* (Technical report). London: Middlesex University.

Groenewald, C., Wong, W. B. L., Attfield, S., Passmore, P., & Kodagoda, N. (2017a). How analysts think: Navigating uncertainty – Aspirations, considerations and strategies. In *Proceedings of the 13th International Conference on Naturalistic Decision Making* (pp. 56–64). Bath. Available at: https://www.researchgate.net/profile/Julie_Gore/publication/320146441_Naturalistic_Decision_Making_and_Uncertainty_Proceedings_of_the_13th_Bi-Annual_Naturalistic_Decision_Making_Conference_University_of_Bath_UK/links/59d0aeb30f7e9b4fd7f9fcbf/Naturalistic-Decision-Making-and-Uncertainty-Proceedings-of-the-13th-Bi-Annual-Naturalistic-Decision-Making-Conference-University-of-Bath-UK.pdf

Groenewald, C., Wong, W. B. L., Attfield, S., Passmore, P., & Kodagoda, N. (2017b). How analysts think: How do criminal intelligence analysts recognise and manage significant information? In *Proceedings of the European Intelligence and Security Informatics Conference (EISIC) 2017*, Dekelia Air Base, Attica, Greece. IEEE 2017.

Hammond, K. R., Hamm, R. M., Grassia, J., & Pearson, T. (1987). Direct comparison of the efficacy of intuitive and analytical cognition in expert judgment. *IEEE Transactions on Systems, Man, and Cybernetics, 17*(5), 753–770.

HMIC. (2015). *HMIC – Building the picture – An inspection of police information management.* Available at: https://www.justiceinspectorates.gov.uk/hmic/publications/building-picture-an-inspection-of-police-information-management/

Kahneman, D. (2011). *Thinking, fast and slow*. London: Allen Lane.

Klein, G., & Klinger, D. (1991). *Naturalistic decision making*. Available at: http://www.au.af.mil/au/awc/awcgate/decision/nat-dm.pdf

Klein, G. A., Calderwood, R., & Clinton-Cirocco, A. (1986, September). Rapid decision making on the fire ground. In *Proceedings of the Human Factors Society Annual Meeting* (Vol. 30, No. 6, pp. 576–580). Sage/Los Angeles: SAGE Publications.

Klein, G., Ross, K. G., Moon, B. M., Klein, D. E., Hoffman, R. R., & Hollnagel, E. (2003). Macrocognition. *IEEE Intelligent Systems, 18*(3), 81–85.

Klein, G., Feltovich, P. J., Bradshaw, J. M., & Woods, D. D. (2005). Common ground and coordination in joint activity. *Organizational Simulation, 53*, 139–184.

Klein G., Phillips J. K., Rall E. L., & Peluso D. A. (2007). A data-frame theory of sensemaking. In R. R. Hoffman (Ed.), *Expertise Out of Context Proceedings of the Sixth International Conference on NDM* (pp. 113–155). Erlbaum.

Moore, C., & Dunham, P. J. (Eds.). (1995). *Joint attention: Its origins and role in development.* Hillsdale: Lawrence Erlbaum Associates.

Passmore, P. J., Attfield, S., Kodagoda, N., Groenewald, C., & Wong, B. W. (2015, September). Supporting the externalisation of thinking in criminal intelligence analysis. In *Intelligence and Security Informatics Conference (EISIC), 2015 European* (pp. 16–23). IEEE.

Pennington, N., & Hastie, R. (1992). Explaining the evidence: Tests of the story model for juror decision making. *Journal of Personality and Social Psychology, 62*(2), 189.

Pirolli, P., & Card, K. (2005). The sensemaking process and leverage points for analyst technology as identified through cognitive task analysis. In *Conference: Proceedings of International Conference on Intelligence Analysis.* Available at: https://www.researchgate.net/publication/215439203_The_sensemaking_process_and_leverage_points_for_Analyst_technology_as_identified_through_cognitive_task_analysis

Rao, S. (2003). Making sense of making stories: Law, literature, life. *Law Library Journal, 95*, 455.

Rooney, C., Attfield, S., Wong, B. W., & Choudhury, S. (2014). INVISQUE as a tool for intelligence analysis: The construction of explanatory narratives. *International Journal of Human-Computer Interaction, 30*(9), 703–717.

Segel, E., & Heer, J. (2010). Narrative visualization: Telling stories with data. *IEEE Transactions on Visualization and Computer Graphics, 16*(6), 1139–1148.

Selvaraj, N., Attfield, S., Passmore, P., & Wong, B. W. (2016, August). How analysts think: think-steps as a tool for structuring sensemaking in criminal intelligence analysis. In *Intelligence and Security Informatics Conference (EISIC), 2016 European* (pp. 68–75). IEEE.

Toulmin, S. E. (2003). *The uses of argument*. Cambridge: Cambridge University Press.

UNODC. (2011). *UNODC – CI – Manual for analysts*. Vienna: United Nations Office. Available at: https://www.unodc.org/documents/organized-crime/Law-Enforcement/Criminal_Intelligence_for_Analysts.pdf

Wagenaar, W., Koppen, P., & Crombag, H. (1993). *Anchored narratives : The psychology of criminal evidence.* Available at: https://www.researchgate.net/publication/232456113_Anchored_Narratives_The_Psychology_of_Criminal_Evidence

Wigmore, J. H. (1931). The principles of judicial proof or the process of proof as given by logic. In *Psychology, and general experience, and illustrated in judicial trials, 2nd edition*. Boston: Little, Brown and Company.

Wong, B. W. (2014, September). How analysts think (?): Early observations. In *Intelligence and Security Informatics Conference (JISIC), 2014 IEEE Joint* (pp. 296–299). IEEE.

Wong, B. W., & Kodagoda, N. (2016, September). How analysts think: Anchoring, laddering and associations. In *Proceedings of the Human Factors and Ergonomics Society Annual Meeting* (Vol. 60, No. 1, pp. 178–182). Sage/Los Angeles: SAGE Publications.

Chapter 9
Situating Fear of Crime: The Prospects for Criminological Research to Use Smartphone Applications to Gather Experience Sampling Data

Alexander Engström and Karl Kronkvist

Introduction

> Because fear of crime is just a feeling, some might wonder why it is important, particularly as a target for police action. Certainly, crime itself must be more important than mere feelings about crime? (Cordner 2010, p. 1)

Although some may argue that fear of crime is "just a feeling", research indicates that its consequences may be severe, and include negative effects on individual mental health, physical functioning and perceived quality of life (Stafford et al. 2007). Worrying about becoming a victim of a crime may also restrict individuals' daily routines, with them e.g. choosing to stay at home rather than participate in public environment activities, which may in turn have negative effects on community-level crime rates due to decreased informal social control, or fewer "eyes on the street" (Wilson and Kelling 1982; Skogan 1986; Hale 1996). Given the potential negative impact of fear of crime at both the individual and community levels, in addition to the fact that fear is more prevalent in the population than victimisation per se (e.g. Hale 1996; SNCCP 2017), we believe that strategies to reduce fear of crime should be of focal concern in the field of next-generation community policing.[1]

Designing best practice initiatives to reduce fear of crime, however, requires state of the art knowledge on the outcome of interest. Although there is a great deal of

---

[1] A version of this paper was first presented at the Next Generation Community Policing conference held in Heraklion, Greece in October 2017.

A. Engström (✉) · K. Kronkvist
Department of Criminology, Malmö University, Malmö, Sweden
e-mail: alexander.engstrom@mau.se; karl.kronkvist@mau.se

© The Author(s) 2018
G. Leventakis, M. R. Haberfeld (eds.), *Community-Oriented Policing and Technological Innovations*, SpringerBriefs in Criminology,
https://doi.org/10.1007/978-3-319-89294-8_9

literature focused on conceptualisations, definitions and measures of fear of crime (e.g. Ferraro and LaGrange 1987; Ferraro 1995; Farrall et al. 1997; Hough 2004), and also on explanations of fear (e.g. Box et al. 1988; Roman and Chalfin 2008), we have identified two gaps in the knowledge from existing research. First, fear of crime is predominantly studied from a cross-sectional perspective, with respondents being asked, often on a yearly basis using different population samples, to rate their average experiences of fear (e.g. Skogan and Maxfield 1981; Gibson et al. 2002; Brunton-Smith and Sturgis 2011). The widely used cross-sectional approach has restricted the opportunities for examining variations in individual-level fear of crime over time and space, despite the fact that researchers have argued that fear of crime should be studied as a dynamic rather than a static experience (Hale 1996; Pain 1997, 2000). Second, and in line with research on offending (Wikström et al. 2012), we would argue that fear of crime is dependent on individual attributes and experiences in *interaction* with environmental factors. Fear of crime should thus be studied using methods that capture person-setting interactions, i.e. *situations* in which fear of crime is experienced.

The aim of this paper is to present an overview of the *situational fear of crime* concept and of how the technical evolution of smartphones has provided researchers with new tools to gather data that were previously unobtainable. It will be argued that the use of situational research instruments provides knowledge on fear of crime that may be beneficial for both researchers and practitioners. A focus on situational fear of crime does not mean dismissing other approaches to studying fear of crime but is rather one of a number of perspectives that may be employed in the study of this phenomenon. We would argue, however, that previous research has directed insufficient attention at the situational dimension.

Fear of Crime, Situational Dynamics, and Lifestyle-Routine Activities

Research has provided a number of insights into why individuals experience fear of crime. For instance, fear of crime is dependent on individual attributes (such as gender and age) as well as previous experiences of criminal victimisation (see Box et al. 1988; Hale 1996; Pain 2000). Research also demonstrates that fear of crime is correlated with both physical characteristics (such as signs of decay and poor lighting) and social characteristics (such as social networks and cohesion) of the immediate environment (see Lorenc et al. 2012, 2013). Although individual and environmental characteristics are important in the explanation of fear of crime, we believe that there is a black box that still needs to be explored in order to fully understand how the individual-environment nexus generates fear of crime.

Proceeding on the basis of the Situational Action Theory of crime causation, our hypothesis is that fear of crime may be explained by reference to the same mechanisms that are used to explain both participation in crime and criminal victimisation; it is the *interaction* between "kinds of people" and "kinds of settings" that creates *situations* (Wikström et al. 2012) in which fear of crime may be experienced as a *situational phenomenon*. Pain (2000) provides an illustrative example of this conceptual approach when she argues that places are not themselves fear-inducing but rather serve to trigger individuals' internal fears that are related to other factors, for example, women's fear of men. The situation itself consists of the person(s) present, the location in which the situation is played out, and the kind of activity taking place (Pervin 1978). Although a situation involves both the individual and the environment, in the context of the situational approach, it is the interaction between a person and a particular setting within the environment that needs to be examined (Wikström et al. 2012). While researchers have begun to investigate the situational dynamics of offending and victimisation (Wikström et al. 2012; Bernasco et al. 2013; Averdijk and Bernasco 2015), less is known about the situational dynamics of fear of crime (for an exception see Solymosi et al. 2015).

Situational fear of crime must be understood within a theoretical framework that allows for situational explanations. Situational Action Theory explains individual actions (i.e. why individuals act as they do either after deliberation or habitually), and other, non-action based theories are therefore needed as a complement if we are to understand outcomes other than actions (e.g. victimisation and fear of crime). Lifestyle-Exposure Theory explains how risky lifestyles lead to some people being more exposed to environments in which victimisation is more likely to occur (Hindelang et al. 1978), while Routine Activities Theory describes what it is that makes environments criminogenic (Cohen and Felson 1979). These theories are commonly merged into a Lifestyle-Routine Activities Theory (McNeeley 2015) and are compatible as a result of their shared focus on criminal opportunities or crime incidents. Similarly, Lifestyle-Routine Activities Theory may assist in understanding why people are exposed to situations which contain known fear-generating cues ("opportunities for fear"). These fear-generating cues may, for instance, be related to Routine Activities Theory's basic explanation of the factors required for a crime to occur, once we introduce a tweak to capture the subjective fear experience; fear is more likely when a *perceived suitable target* coincides in time and space with a *perceived motivated offender* in the *perceived absence of capable guardians* (for the original formulation, see Cohen and Felson 1979). Further, and perhaps more importantly, Lifestyle-Routine Activities Theory may also contribute to a greater understanding of how people with *different lifestyles* perceive *similar situational cues*. It is not unlikely that a study of the fear of crime that focuses on the person-setting interaction may reveal that individuals who are highly exposed to situations that the literature defines as fear-generating are in fact less fearful as a result of their knowledge of and habituation to these kinds of situations.

Importantly, lifestyle was originally operationalised via various proxy measures, such as age and gender (e.g. Hindelang et al. 1978) which is clearly not linked to any form of situational methodology. More recent studies have employed a somewhat more refined operationalisation of lifestyle, but they still generally omit actual situational measures (e.g. Schreck et al. 2002; Svensson and Pauwels 2010).

A situational measure of lifestyle must capture the true essence of a lifestyle as it is manifested in various situations; in the interactions between a person and the environment. When fear of crime is studied in terms of the units in which it is experienced (situations), it may be possible to unravel the mediating effect of lifestyles on the historically demonstrated connections between proxy measures and levels of fear. There is research that points in this direction (see Mesch 2000), although it has not employed a genuine situational approach.

Measuring Situational Dynamics and Lifestyle-Routine Activities Using Smartphones

To capture the essence of the person-setting interaction, one must be able to gather information not only on individuals, but also on the *time*, *place*, and *content* of a specific setting. In previous research on the situational dynamics of crime causation, the Space-Time Budget interview has been proposed as a viable means of retrospectively charting respondents' everyday activities in detail (for details see Wikström et al. 2012; Hoeben et al. 2014). The Space-Time Budget has however been subject to criticisms linked to problems of memory bias, concerns related to the size of the time-slots employed and the possibility of capturing uncommon events such as offending, victimisation (Hoeben et al. 2014) and thus potentially also experiences of fear of crime. Another methodological approach, which may not suffer from these potential flaws when it comes to gathering self-reported situational data, is the Experience Sampling Method (ESM) (Larson and Csikszentmihalyi 1983). ESM enables researchers to study activity patterns in individuals' everyday lives (e.g. Kahneman et al. 2004) with activities, feelings, and emotions, for example, being captured as they occur at a specific point in time and space (Larson and Csikszentmihalyi 1983). The methodology requires a signalling device to alert participants and a questionnaire that the participant fills in at the moment of the alert, which originally took the form of a personal pager and a paper questionnaire (Csikszentmihalyi and Larson 1987).

The emergence of smartphones has revolutionised the ESM procedure for a number of reasons. The smartphone releases respondents from the burden of using additional paraphernalia (e.g. pagers and paper questionnaires) since the phone itself contains these functionalities, and most individuals own a device since the smartphone has become an "integrated part of the lives of most people in Western countries" (Raento et al. 2009, p. 427). A smartphone application can notify the respondent by sending a push notification, making the person aware that it is time to answer one or more questions in a built-in, short questionnaire (see Gaggioli et al. 2013). In addition, a smartphone application can quite easily gather latent time and geo data using built-in smartphone functions. This ability to gather latent data is also likely to provide more accurate information on time and location than self-reported data, as well as easing the burden of participation since these data are collected automatically. Finally, smartphone applications also provide the researcher with numerous possibilities for the use of systematic procedures. For instance, notifications to respondents may be sent at random points in time, within specific time-slots (e.g. morning, mid-day, afternoon, or evening) (Solymosi et al. 2015), or when respondents enter a geo-fenced area of interest (a specific neighbourhood, a shopping area, or similar) (Chataway et al. 2017).

The ESM approach based on the use of smartphones has been successfully employed in several studies, which have, for example, examined variations in individual emotions such as happiness and stress over space and time (MacKerron and Mourato 2013; Sonck and Fernee 2013; Shoval et al. 2018). To our knowledge, however, only two published studies have examined fear of crime as a situational event using the ESM approach in combination with smartphone applications. In one pioneering ESM study, Solymosi et al. (2015) argue that fear of crime should be viewed as an event rather than an abstract long-term experience. They studied whether fear of crime varies between and within individuals both over the course of the day and between different places. The study participants were alerted at random times, up to four times each day, over a 30-day period, and were asked to answer a few short questions regarding their worries about becoming a victim of a crime at that specific moment. In addition, the application gathered relevant spatial data and the time of the report.

The other ESM study on fear of crime (Chataway et al. 2017) used a somewhat different approach. Instead of notifying respondents at random times during the day, Chataway and colleagues alerted the participants at specific places. Having first geo-fenced ten areas (e.g. shopping areas, beaches, etc.), the participants were notified as they entered these zones, which was detected by the built-in GPS sensor in their smartphones. In addition, instead of simply asking a short question on the experience of fear of crime, Chataway and colleagues employed a much larger questionnaire focused on four dimensions of fear of crime, which had been inspired by the work of Jackson (2005). Further, in addition to the study gathering auxiliary spatial and temporal data on the responses, the participants were also asked to assess their immediate environment (e.g. disorder, perceived informal social control) when they received a notification.

Although based on small numbers of participants, these studies confirm that an ESM approach to fear of crime is possible. For instance, Solymosi et al. (2015) found support for inter- and intra-individual variations in fear of crime; in fact, the participants were most often not afraid at all, but when fear was experienced, it varied in space and time and was particularly concentrated to specific geographic hotspots. However, the most important contribution of the two ESM studies to the research on fear of crime lies in the way they have challenged the current knowledge base.

Locating Fear in Place, Time and Situation: The Prospects for Future Research

In this paper we have argued that fear of crime should be viewed and studied as a situational experience. Building on well-established criminological theory, we believe that the person-setting interaction constitutes the key element for a situational approach. By expanding our understanding of situational fear of crime we may also advance towards the next generation of fear-reducing strategies. This would involve not only focusing strategies on place and time, but also on the interactions between individuals and their environments, in which place and time may of course play an important, but not exclusive role, in the emergence of fear.

We also believe, however, that despite their major contribution as pioneering studies, the two existing studies on situational fear of crime do not fully capture situational dynamics in an entirely appropriate way. Although both studies gather relevant situational data on time and place, time and place must not be confounded with situation. Chataway et al. (2017) supplement the geographical location with additional relevant characteristics relating to the area concerned, but these variables (in addition to time) only represent some of the elements of a situation. The ESM approach in general, however, is highly relevant for studying the person-setting interaction; it offers the ability to understand the actual situational cues that are important in the person-setting interaction.

Further, a situational perspective on fear of crime needs to be based on a sound theoretical framework, as is the case with any credible explanation of any phenomenon. We have argued that conceptions drawn from Situational Action Theory and Lifestyle-Routine Activities Theory may constitute a foundation from which our hypotheses on situational fear of crime can be tested. This is not to say that other theories of fear of crime lack importance, but is rather intended to show the potential of established criminological theories in the context of this endeavour. Research instruments that use an ESM approach in combination with our suggested theoretical framework may provide insights that will help the research field move forward by addressing largely unanswered questions regarding intra- and interpersonal variations in fear across space and time. The main benefit of adding an adequate theoretical foundation is that this should allow us to actually explain situational fear of crime rather than merely describing it. We believe that Situational Action Theory and Lifestyle-Routine Activities Theory may explain the mechanisms that are present prior to and during person-setting interactions, since it may explain both which persons find themselves in certain situations, and how different people perceive the same situations.

Finally, and perhaps most importantly, it is essential to emphasise the potential for the wider use of research tools that employ an ESM methodology. These tools may be relevant outside the academic sphere because they allow for the more direct measurement of situational phenomena. It is thus not surprising that the ESM approach has been proposed as a highly relevant tool for policy makers in many different areas (MacKerron and Mourato 2013). We maintain that fear of crime is one such area because situational research on fear of crime is highly relevant both for public agencies, such as law enforcement agencies, and private organisations that are involved in fear reduction programmes. We urge the research community to adopt a situational approach to the study of fear of crime. We would encourage the use of such an approach both to explore the technological possibilities of employing an ESM methodology, and to provide relevant theoretical explanations when fear of crime is examined. Improved understanding provides a basis for better solutions, which may in turn have practical implications for the development of safer urban communities.

References

Averdijk, M., & Bernasco, W. (2015). Testing the situational explanation of victimization among adolescents. *Journal of Research in Crime and Delinquency, 52*(2), 151–180.

Bernasco, W., Ruiter, S., Bruinsma, G. J. N., Pauwels, L. J. R., & Weerman, F. M. (2013). Situational causes of offending: A fixed-effects analysis of space-time budget data. *Criminology, 51*(4), 895–926.

Box, S., Hale, C., & Andrews, G. (1988). Explaining fear of crime. *British Journal of Criminology, 28*(3), 340–356.

Brunton-Smith, I., & Sturgis, P. (2011). Do neighborhoods generate fear of crime? An empirical test using the British Crime Survey. *Criminology, 49*(2), 331–369.

Chataway, M. L., Hart, T. C., Coomber, R., & Bond, C. (2017). The geography of crime fear: A pilot study exploring event-based perceptions of risk using mobile technology. *Applied Geography, 86*, 300–307.

Cohen, L. E., & Felson, M. (1979). Social change and crime rate trends: A routine activity approach. *American Sociological Review, 44*(4), 588–608.

Cordner, G. (2010). *Reducing fear of crime: Strategies for police.* Washington, DC: US Department of Justice/Office of Community Oriented Policing Services.

Csikszentmihalyi, M., & Larson, R. (1987). Validity and reliability of the experience-sampling method. *The Journal of Nervous and Mental Disease, 175*(9), 526–536.

Farrall, S., Bannister, J., Ditton, J., & Gilchrist, E. (1997). Questioning the measurement of the 'fear of crime': Findings from a major methodological study. *British Journal of Criminology, 37*(4), 658–679.

Ferraro, K. F. (1995). *Fear of crime: Interpreting victimization risk.* Albany: State University of New York Press.

Ferraro, K. F., & LaGrange, R. (1987). The measurement of fear of crime. *Sociological Inquiry, 57*(1), 70–97.

Gaggioli, A., Pioggia, G., Tartarisco, G., Baldus, G., Corda, D., Cipresso, P., & Riva, G. (2013). A mobile data collection platform for mental health research. *Personal and Ubiquitous Computing, 17*(2), 241–251.

Gibson, C. L., Zhao, J., Lovrich, N. P., & Gaffney, M. J. (2002). Social integration, individual perceptions of collective efficacy, and fear of crime in three cities. *Justice Quarterly, 19*(3), 537–564.

Hale, C. (1996). Fear of crime: A review of the literature. *International Review of Victimology, 4*, 79–150.

Hindelang, M. J., Gottfredson, M. R., & Garofalo, J. (1978). *Victims of personal crime: An empirical foundation for a theory of personal victimization.* Cambridge, MA: Ballinger.

Hoeben, M., Bernasco, W., Weerman, F. M., Pauwels, L., & van Halem, S. (2014). The space-time budget method in criminological research. *Crime Science, 3*(12), 1–15.

Hough, M. (2004). Worry about crime: Mental events or mental states? *International Journal of Social Research Methodology, 7*(2), 173–176.

Jackson, J. (2005). Validating new measures of the fear of crime. *International Journal of Social Research Methodology, 8*(4), 297–315.

Kahneman, D., Krueger, A. B., Schkade, D. A., Schwarz, N., & Stone, A. A. (2004). A survey method for characterizing daily life experience: The day reconstruction method. *Science, 306*(5702), 1776–1780.

Larson, R., & Csikszentmihalyi, M. (1983). The experience sampling method. *New Directions for Methodology of Social & Behavioral Science, 15*, 41–56.

Lorenc, T., Clayton, S., Neary, D., Whitehead, M., Petticrew, M., Thomson, H., Cummins, S., Sowden, A., & Renton, A. (2012). Crime, fear of crime, environment, and mental health and wellbeing: Mapping review of theories and causal pathways. *Health & Place, 18*(4), 757–765.

Lorenc, T., Petticrew, M., Whitehead, M., Neary, D., Clayton, S., Wright, K., Thomson, H., Cummins, S., Sowden, A., & Renton, A. (2013). Fear of crime and the environment: Systematic review of UK qualitative evidence. *BMC Public Health, 13*(1), 496–503.

MacKerron, G., & Mourato, S. (2013). Happiness is greater in natural environments. *Global Environmental Change, 23*(5), 992–1000.

McNeeley, S. (2015). Lifestyle-routine activities and crime events. *Journal of Contemporary Criminal Justice, 31*(1), 30–52.

Mesch, G. S. (2000). Perceptions of risk, lifestyle activities, and fear of crime. *Deviant Behavior, 21*(1), 47–62.

Pain, R. H. (1997). 'Old age' and ageism in urban research: The case of fear of crime. *International Journal of Urban and Regional Research, 21*(1), 117–128.

Pain, R. H. (2000). Place, social relations and the fear of crime: A review. *Progress in Human Geography, 24*(3), 365–387.

Pervin, L. A. (1978). Definitions, measurements, and classifications of stimuli, situations, and environments. *Human Ecology, 6*(1), 71–105.

Raento, M., Oulasvirta, A., & Eagle, N. (2009). Smartphones: An emerging tool for social scientists. *Sociological Methods & Research, 37*(3), 426–454.

Roman, C. G., & Chalfin, A. (2008). Fear of walking outdoors: A multilevel ecologic analysis of crime and disorder. *American Journal of Preventive Medicine, 34*(4), 306–312.

Schreck, C. J., Wright, R. A., & Miller, J. M. (2002). A study of individual and situational antecedents of violent victimization. *Justice Quarterly, 19*(1), 159–180.

Shoval, N., Schvimer, Y., & Tamir, M. (2018). Tracking technologies and urban analysis: Adding the emotional dimension. *Cities, 72*, 34–42.

Skogan, W. G. (1986). The fear of crime and its behavioral implications. In E. A. Fattah (Ed.), *From crime policy to victim policy. Reorienting the justice system* (pp. 167–188). London: Macmillan Press.

Skogan, W., & Maxfield, M. (1981). *Coping with crime: Individual and neighborhood reactions.* Beverly Hills: Sage Publications.

Solymosi, R., Bowers, K., & Fujiyama, T. (2015). Mapping fear of crime as a context-dependent everyday experience that varies in space and time. *Legal and Criminological Psychology, 20*(2), 193–211.

Sonck, N., & Fernee, H. (2013). *Using smartphones in survey research: A multifunctional tool. Implementation of a time use app; a feasability study.* The Hague: The Netherlands Institute for Social Research (SCP).

Stafford, M., Chandola, T., & Marmot, M. (2007). Association between fear of crime and mental health and physical functioning. *American Journal of Public Health, 97*(11), 2076–2081.

Svensson, R., & Pauwels, L. (2010). Is a risky lifestyle always "risky"? The interaction between individual propensity and lifestyle risk in adolescent offending: A test in two urban samples. *Crime & Delinquency, 56*(4), 608–626.

Swedish National Council for Crime Prevention [SNCCP]. (2017). *Swedish Crime Survey 2016. English summary of Brå-report 2017:1*. Stockholm: The Swedish National Council for Crime Prevention.

Wikström, P. O. H., Oberwittler, D., Treiber, K., & Hardie, B. (2012). *Breaking rules: The social and situational dynamics of young people's urban crime*. Oxford: Oxford University Press.

Wilson, J. Q., & Kelling, G. L. (1982, March). The police and neighborhood safety: Broken windows. *Atlantic Monthly*, pp. 29–38.

Chapter 10
Analytic Provenance as Constructs of Behavioural Markers for Externalizing Thinking Processes in Criminal Intelligence Analysis

Junayed Islam, B. L. William Wong, and Kai Xu

Introduction

Visual Analytics tools in the recent years have made an impact in the criminal intelligence and analysis communities. Histories of user interactions known as Analytic Provenance have been used to advance our understanding of tool usage and user goals in a variety of areas. User interaction histories contain information about the sequence of choices that analysts make when exploring data or performing a task. To understand how the analyses are being made it requires support of correlating lower-level events during analysis process with upper level sub-tasks, tasks and goals of decision making process as proposed by Gotz and Zhou (2008).

Until recently, most of the research has focused on the techniques and methods for refining visual analytic tools, with the emphasis on empowering analysts to make discoveries faster and more accurately. Although this emphasis is relevant and necessary, we argue that the process through which an analyst arrives at the conclusion is just as important as the discoveries themselves. Understanding how an analyst performs a successful criminal investigation will finally let us start bridging the gap between the art of analysis and the science of analytics. We found out from the detection approach of behavioural marker from analytical data that they can bridge such gap alongside of performance measurement. The overarching aims of this research are based on following research questions to find out-.

J. Islam (✉) · B. L. William Wong
Interaction Design Centre, Middlesex University, London, UK
e-mail: j.islam@mdx.ac.uk; w.wong@mdx.ac.uk

K. Xu
Department of Computer Science, Middlesex University, London, UK
e-mail: k.xu@mdx.ac.uk

© The Author(s) 2018
G. Leventakis, M. R. Haberfeld (eds.), *Community-Oriented Policing and Technological Innovations*, SpringerBriefs in Criminology,
https://doi.org/10.1007/978-3-319-89294-8_10

RQ1:   What are the constructs of behavioural markers for criminal intelligence analysis?

RQ2:   How to externalize analyst's thinking processes from constructs of behavioural markers in criminal intelligence analysis?

This contribution is part of a research work aimed to find out appropriate methods or techniques to evaluate a visual analytic tool named as Analyst's User Interface (AUI) of the project VALCRI[1] (Visual Analytics for Sensemaking in Criminal Intelligence Analysis). In section "Related Works" numbers of existing related work, in section "Development Approach of Behavioural Marker System" methodology overview to find out Behavioural Markers (BMs), their constructs and detection approaches have been presented. Section "Conclusion" includes conclusion and future work.

Related Works

Behavioural Marker systems are now being developed for performance measurement in a range of organizational settings, especially in high reliability industries such as air aviation, nuclear power, maritime transport, and medicine. They are usually structured into a set of categories (e.g. co-operation, decision making, and situational awareness). Normally, these categories are then sub-divided into more specific nontechnical skills or elements. The seminal research on behavioural markers comes from studies of civilian pilots carried out by Helmreich and colleagues at the University of Texas. In the late 1980s they developed a data collection form called the LINE/LOS Checklist (LLC) to gather information on flight crews' crew resource management performance (Helmreich et al. 1990). This checklist has been used as the basis of many airlines' behavioural marker systems (Flin and Martin 2001). Behavioural Markers (BMs) concept is not only used to measure team performance in aviation or medical sectors but also their uses for evaluating visualization are noticeable. North (2006) claims that the purpose of visualization is insight and to determine to what degree visualizations achieve this purpose. He listed some of the characteristics of insight such as – complex, deep, qualitative, unexpected and relevant. Saraiya et al. (2005) defined insight as an individual observation about the data, a unit of discovery. They presented several characteristics of insight while running a pilot study on biological and microarray data such as – observation, time, domain value, hypotheses, directed versus unexpected, breadth and depth, category. In a case study with the popular visual analytics application Jigsaw, Kang et al. (2009) found that analysts' interaction histories showed evidence of the high-level sensemaking processes (Pirolli and Card 2005). Reda et al. (2014) approached interaction and sensemaking by combining interaction logs and user-reported mental processes into an extended log and modeling the log using transition diagrams to better understand the transition between mental and interaction states.

---

[1] VALCRI – http://valcri.org/

Development Approach of Behavioural Marker System

The typical method for the initial development of behavioural marker systems is to carry out a literature review of previous domain specific research concerned with nontechnical skills, followed by interviews with subject matter experts designed to extract the nontechnical skills required to do their job effectively (e.g. Fletcher et al. 2004; Mitchell and Flin 2009; Yule et al. 2006). We also carried out a systematic literature review by using several electronic databases (PsychINFO, ScienceDirect, Web of Science, Google Scholar, and the Defence Technical Information Center) to identify research articles with search terms: criminal intelligence, behavioural markers, human factors, situation awareness, decision making, intelligence analyst, cognitive skills etc. We considered cognitive attributes to present our phase-1 (Flin et al. 2008) behavioural markers found from literature review. We also arranged a workshop to discuss different concepts and extract related cognitive behaviours. There were about 30 criminal intelligence domain experts present in the workshop including ex-police, ex-intelligence analysts, researchers and other developers. The whole team was divided into several groups and then each concept was gone through one by one. Each person in the group said some words that they associated with the concept. We put them all on post-its and organized them thematically (i.e, an affinity diagram) at the end. Thus we formed an exhaustive list of behavioural markers for criminal intelligence analyst as shown in Table 10.1. Our aim was to identify a set of mostly relevant behavioural markers by considering human factors and cognitive engineering principles that underlie the design of user interface, visualization and interaction on criminal intelligence analysis system. The goal is to determine the extent to which imagination, insight, transparency and fluidity & rigour are enhanced on the assumption that improving these, will likely improve analysts' ability to solve crime or be better at performing criminal intelligence analysis by using Analyst's User Interface (AUI) of the project VALCRI (Wong et al. 2014).

Detection Method

From a quantitative behavioural developmental theory perspective (Commons et al. 1998), behavioural constructs are events that have the potential to be directly observed. We have defined a set of behavioural markers into Table 10.1, and mainly look for their occurrence in the recorded analytic process data by considering the context of the situations that these behaviours were observed (i.e. before and after actions and conditions). Within such task environment in criminal intelligence, process data from the task interface allows for the collection of information that may be indicative of observable behaviours. So, the challenges underlies of

Table 10.1 Constructs of observable behaviours in criminal intelligence analysis

Categories	Antecedents	Processes	Outcomes
Imagination	Passion, inspired, moral **Motivation** Openness, focused, inspiration, motivation, playfulness, curiosity, freedom	**Divergent thinking** Openness, curiosity, creative play, exploring, experimenting, idea generation, free thinking, freedom, outlier thinking, thinking outside the box, inventing, going beyond given information, traditional assumptions, unusual interpretation, fluency, flexibility **Mental modelling** Analytical reasoning, metaphorical thinking, analogical reasoning, moral reasoning, contrarian thinking, probability reasoning, questioning, abstraction of terms, changing potential output, comparison, finding alternate objects, generating hypotheses, scenario building, inferring possibilities	Idea generation, novelty, inventive, abstraction of terms, acceptance
Insight	Incubation, flair, reason, belief in truth, getting out of an impass **Means to support insight** Visualized information, visualizing information **Managing complexity** Untangling complexity, mess finding.	**Ideational** Developing new ideas, developing new perspective, evolving perception, revelation, intuition, understanding a situation, perceiving information, laddering, creating a new pattern, associative questioning, leap of faith **Problem solving** Recognition and discovery, problem reformulation, reframing, uncovering	**Consequences** Relevance enhanced perception, being able to explain, contribution to plausible narrative, evidence for hypothesis building, verifying hypothesis, contradiction of previous beliefs, questioning assumptions **Outputs** Awareness, understanding, enhanced perception, unexpected understanding, sudden jump in understanding, understanding hypothesis, A solution of unknown provenance, new knowledge, new pattern, possibility, discard options, breakthrough

Transparency	**Proper motivation** Making awareness visible	Structured analysis, critical thinking, assessment of source quality, open source, ease of access, see through, observability, recording of provenance, externalization of reasoning, externalization of assumptions	**Experience of giving insight** Seeing something in a different light, unexpected understanding, eureka moment, recognition and discovery, without conscious thoughts, internal and conscious
			Accountability and legal compliance Showing compliance, accountability, legal clarity, legal certainty, fairness, honesty, truth
	Techniques Usability, visibility and configurability of algorithmic parameters, immune to changes by unauthorized persons, showing info outside threshold, define user access. User manuals	**Precision on communication** Communication of uncertainty, communication of complexity, communication of probability, communication of limitations, communication of analytic confidence, communication of analytic confidence	**Effects** Contradiction of privacy, structured analysis, analytic provenance, making awareness visible, critical thinking, acknowledging alternatives, ability to understand and reconstruct operations or decisions
			Auditability Feedback, easy to access, open source, disclosure, traceability, ability know and track back, verifiability, showing information outside of threshold, direct manipulation
		Engagement of multiple stakeholders Individual and collaborative roles, different stakeholders	**Provenance** Audit, traceability, disclosure of algorithmic reasoning, accountability, elements & paths between premises & conclusions in reasoning
			Precision Counters misuse, not ambiguous, not beguiling. Clarity, accuracy, certainty, see through, applicability, acknowledging alternatives, quality of information

Table 10.1 (continued)

Categories	Antecedents	Processes	Outcomes
Rigour	**Visual support** Clear distinction between facts and suppositions, narration. **Analytic support** Application of analytic techniques, helpfulness, decision point, seeing the process of deepening analysis	**Rigour in analysis** Structured analytic technique, consideration of multiple hypothesis, critical thinking, accuracy of judgement, stick to rules & procedures, principle, order, responsibility, due diligence, attention to detail, information validation, adherence to standards, rigour of provenance, certainty, assessment of sources & quality, timeliness, substantiate **Rigour in the communication of analytic findings** Communication of analytical provenance, communication of analytic confidence, communication of assumptions, communication of probabilities, communication of uncertainty, rigour of argument, evidenced, substantiate, trust calibration, confirmative hypothesis, decision point, information validation	**Compliance** Due diligence, responsibility, legal compliance, adherence to standards, assessment of sources and quality, comprehensiveness, thorough, thoughtfulness, attention to detail, exhaustive, certainty, stick to rules and procedures, order, rigour of process, principles, rigour of provenance **Fit for purpose** Timeliness, relevance, commitment **Transparency** Clear distinction between Facts & Suppositions, clarity of reasoning, transparency, externalization of reasoning process, seeing the process of deepening analysis, rigour of provenance, communication of analytical provenance
Fluidity	**Visual support** Adaptable UI, intuitive interactions, rapidly reversible interaction, low cognitive load, dynamic, content related adaptation, ease of use, multiple views to blend, transposition of data, variability of logical relationships, fast analytic response time **Analytic support** Transposition of data, no data wrangling, ease of representing relationships, holistic view of data	**Visual support** Intuitive interactions, variability of logical relationships. **Withholding commitment** Circumspect, tentative, malleability, Explorable data analysis, ease of transition, consideration of multiple hypothesis, playfulness	Variability of logical relationships, context related adaptation, ease of use, divergent thinking, Explorable data analysis, playfulness, malleability

converting such analytic process related data into behavioural markers. Within the intelligence analysis environment, process data from the task interface allows for the collection of information that may be indicative of behavioural markers. Such as – Fluency, specifically during the data finding process, can be defined as the ability to generate many different pieces of data. Fluency in data finding is the indicative of a behavioural marker known as "creativity". Imagination can be considered in terms of creativity, and creativity in the literature can be approximated as 'divergent thinking', and researchers have attempted to measure divergent thinking through concepts such as 'fluency in data finding' or 'flexibility unshifting between approach' (Fontenot 1992). This concept of reducing complex construct into simpler, easier to measure constituent cognitive components can be conceivably applied to complex problem solving tasks. Such reductionist approach gives an overview of behavioural markers and their role for the scientists to recognize them when certain behaviours have occurred into analytic process data stream. Data reductions are accomplished through coding and manual interpretation during qualitative research approach, which is extremely labour intensive. Direct observation through video, physical observation, participant interview, audio recording are needed for this purpose.

Action Sequences Computation

The streams of actions during analytic process can be meaningful markers for complex behaviours. Current approaches such as – finite state systems for fixed manipulable elements, a priori establishment of fixed sequences for clearly defined tasks, exhausting all possible sequences for tasks with unpredictable human elements, are available for information computation about behavioural and cognitive processes and their implications for large scale complex analysis. The use of network graph visualization in this context can be a useful exploratory process, rather than exhaustive, to observe and gain understanding which empirical action combinations may provide meaningful sequence for targeted behavioural marker. The sequences need to be converted into a structure that is more suitable for network analysis and visualization. Some sequences might be observed more often while others are only observed in very rare occasions. Low Level Action sequence *Seq. #001* $A \rightarrow B \rightarrow D \rightarrow E \rightarrow G$ as shown in Fig. 10.1, comprises of analytic states A, B, D, E, G are different analytic states after low level actions have been applied on. As we aim to follow a compositionally reductive framework for the contextual information of complex analytic states, we can denote each of them as semantic state composition function $P(S)$ where S is an analytical state.

$$\text{So, } P(S) = S.$$

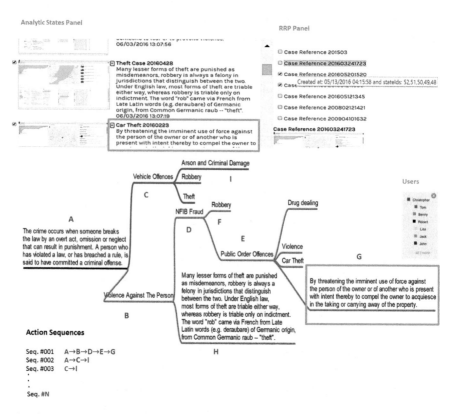

Fig. 10.1 An analytic path showing annotations set by analysts with captured states & their relationships based on interactions with colour coded users (analysts) information. States can be selected from States Panel & RRP list of Analyst's User Interface (AUI) to load analytic path for understanding intersections of analytical states captured by different analysts during their analysis process (Islam et al. 2016)

For *Seq. #001,* it can expressed as –

$$P(S_A) = S_A$$

$$P(S_B) = S_B$$

$$P(S_D) = S_D$$

$$\ldots \quad \ldots \quad \ldots \quad \ldots$$

$P(S_n) = S_n$, where n is the number of nodes.

Thus we computed n th state S_n as $P : S_{A, B, D, \ldots, n-1} \rightarrow S_n$. Composition function of different analytic states can be expressed as –

$$P(S_A) \circ P(S_B) = P \circ P(S_A, S_B) = \{S_A, S_B\} = S_{A,B} \ P : S_A \rightarrow S_B$$

$$P(S_B) \circ P(S_D) = P \circ P(S_B, S_D) = \{S_B, S_D\} = S_{B,D} \ P : S_B \rightarrow S_D$$

$$\ldots \ \ldots \ \ldots \ \ldots \ \ldots \ \ldots \ \ldots$$

$$P \circ P\left(S_{A,B,D,\ldots,n-1}, S_n\right) = \{S_A, S_B, \ldots, S_n\}$$

$P : S_{A, B, D, \ldots, n-1} \rightarrow S_n = S_{ST}$, where S_{ST} is a Sub-Task State (Gotz and Zhou 2008) through low level actions or events.

This is how other low level action sequences *Seq. #002, Seq. #003, ..., ..., ..., Seq. #N* can be computed.

To determine which sequences are more valid measures of 'Behavioural Markers', we consider attributes of Table 10.1 and this would entail some form of network analysis; so each low level actions (representing an analytic state) can be defined as a 'node' and the links that make up a sequence across the nodes can be defined as 'edges'. Eigenvector centrality is one method of computing the "centrality", or approximate importance, of each node in a graph network. The assumption is that each node's centrality is the sum of the centrality values of the nodes that it is connected to. The adjacency and centrality matrices for the action sequence graph as shown in Fig. 10.1 have been computed. The centrality matrix is an eigenvector of the adjacency matrix such that all of its elements are positive. While nodes with higher importance and associated edges indicate that they are taken more often, and therefore may imply that the analysts are finding more sensible choices for shifting from one approach to another (Flexibility) or generating more alternative approaches (Fluency). Creativity is manifested through the flexibility, fluency and originality of responses to a task (Torrance 1988) which can be approximated as 'divergent thinking' or alternately "Imagination".

Conclusion

This research aims to explain how human cognition leads to interactions and vice versa to achieve certain goal. The identified behavioural markers (Table 10.1) are aimed to use as attributes for performance measurement of an Analyst's User Interface (AUI) for the project VALCRI.[1] One of the requirements from a focus group during our previous study (Islam et al. 2016) with the end-users (Police Analysts) was to capture analyst's thinking processes during their analysis. It is difficult to recover such thinking processes by using extended analytical provenance log or only by observing. For example, knowing when one reasoning process ends and another begins may be unclear from a sequence of interaction alone. In our previous research we proposed a captured logical state composition approach and their grouping arrangement (Fig. 10.1) as the solution to cognitive steps sequencing problem along with analytic data. In this research work we have aimed to couple these cognitive steps with analytic data. Endert et al. (2015) contend that a new methodology to couple the cognitive and computational components of visual analytic system is necessary. We have proposed markers of behaviours as attributes for coupling human cognition and analytic computation through interactions. Our eigenvector centrality computation approach by using adjacency matrix of different captured analytic states through low level interactions provides a simple solution of overcoming tedious effort of qualitative approach to detect behavioural markers from sequential actions into analytic provenance dataset.

As for our future work we also aim to conduct an in-depth evaluation study with our end-users to investigate how transitions among behavioural markers can be detected as well as their influences on analytical activities. Analysis of combinations of such behavioural markers that occur during large complex task also introduces research challenges of predictive analytic goal oriented recommendation for action sequences. The inverse compositional reductionist approach can unfold the process of analysis being carried out to reach a goal. But how can such approach be applied on actual working environment, still requires further research.

Acknowledgments The research results reported here has received funding from the European Union Seventh Framework Programme FP7/2007–2013 through Project VALCRI, European Commission Grant Agreement N° FP7-IP-608142, awarded to Middlesex University and partners.

References

Commons, M. L., Trudeau, E. J., Stein, S. A., Richards, F. A., & Krause, S. R. (1998). The existence of developmental stages as shown by the hierarchical complexity of tasks. *Developmental Review, 8*, 237–278.

Endert, A., Chang, R., North, C., & Zhou, M. (2015, July–August). Semantic interaction: Coupling cognition and computation through usable interactive analytics. Published in *IEEE Computer Graphics and Applications, 35*(4). INSPEC Accession Number: 15305788.

Fletcher, G., Flin, R., McGeorge, P., Glavin, R., Maran, N., & Patey, R. (2004). Rating nontechnical skills: Developing a behavioral marker system for use in anaesthesia. *Cognition, Technology, and Work, 6*, 165–171.

Flin, R., & Martin, L. (2001). Behavioral markers for CRM: A review of current practice. *International Journal of Aviation Psychology, 11*, 95–118.

Flin, R., O'Connor, P., & Crichton, M. (2008). *Safety at the sharp end: Training nontechnical skills*. Aldershot: Ashgate Publishing Ltd.

Fontenot, A. N. (1992). Effects of training in creativity and creative problem finding upon business people. *The Journal of Social Psychology, 133*(1), 11–22.

Gotz, D., & Zhou, M. X. (2008). Characterizing user's visual analytic activity for insight provenance. In *Proceedings of the IEEE Symposium on Visual Analytics Science and Technology (VAST)* (pp. 123–130).

Helmreich, R., Wilhelm, J., Kello, J., Taggart, E., & Butler, R. (1990). *Reinforcing and evaluating crew resource management: Evaluator/LOS instructor manual*. Austin: NASA/UT/FAA Aerospace Group.

Islam J., Anslow C., Xu K., Wong W., & Zhang L. (2016). Towards analytical provenance visualization for criminal intelligence analysis. In *Proceedings of the EGUK Conference on Computer Graphics & Visual Computing (CGVC)*, Bournemouth, UK.

Kang, Y.-a, Gorg, C., & Stasko, J. (2009). Evaluating visual analytics systems for investigative analysis: Deriving design principles from a case study. In *Visual Analytics Science and Technology, VAST 2009*. IEEE Symposium on (pp. 139–146). IEEE.

Mitchell, L., & Flin, R. (2009). Scrub practitioners' list of intra-operative nontechnical skills-SPLINTS. In R. Flin & L. Mitchell (Eds.), *Safer Surgery* (pp. 67–82). Aldershot: Ashgate Publishing Ltd.

North, C. (2006). Toward measuring visualization insight. *IEEE Computer Graphics and Applications, 26*(3), 6–9.

Pirolli, P., & Card, S. (2005). The sensemaking process and leverage points for analyst technology as identified through cognitive task analysis. In *Proceedings of International Conference on Intelligence Analysis* (Vol. 5).

Reda, K., Johnson, A. E., Leigh, J., & Papka, M. E. (2014). Evaluating user behavior and strategy during visual exploration. In *Proceedings of the Fifth Workshop on Beyond Time and Errors: Novel Evaluation Methods for Visualization* (pp. 41–45). ACM.

Saraiya, P., North, C., & Duca, K. (2005). An insight-based methodology for evaluating bioinformatics visualizations. *IEEE Transactions on Visualization and Computer Graphics, 11*(4), 1–14.

Torrance, E. P. (1988). The nature of creativity as manifest in its testing. In R. J. Sternberg (Ed.), *The nature of creativity: Contemporary psychological perspectives* (pp. 43–75). Cambridge: Cambridge University Press.

Wong, B. L. W., Zhang, L., & Shepherd, I. D. H. (2014). VALCRI: Addressing european needs for information exploitation of large complex data in criminal intelligence analysis. In: *European Data Forum*, Greece.

Yule, S., Flin, R., Paterson-Brown, S., Maran, N., & Rowley, D. (2006). Development of a rating system for surgeons' nontechnical skills. *Medical Education, 50*, 1098–1104.

Chapter 11
Analysis of Suspended Terrorism-Related Content on Social Media

George Kalpakis, Theodora Tsikrika, Ilias Gialampoukidis, Symeon Papadopoulos, Stefanos Vrochidis, and Ioannis Kompatsiaris

Introduction

Several popular social media platforms that emerged during the past decade have revolutionized modern communications among people worldwide cutting across different nationalities, cultures, and residences, and have resulted in the development of online communities providing the means for the open sharing of information. However, due to their broad reach, social media are also being used with subversive intentions. For instance, in recent years they have been employed by terrorist and extremist groups for further supporting their goals of spreading their propaganda, radicalizing new members, and disseminating material targeting potential perpetrators of future attacks. Therefore, online social networks present a digital space of particular interest to governments, law enforcement agencies and social media companies in their effort to suppress terrorism content.

Identifying terrorism-related content in social media is a challenging task. Social media platforms host overwhelming amounts of discussions, posted daily by millions of people, making it practically impossible to detect extremist or terrorism-related content by solely relying on manual inspection performed by content moderators. Therefore, an interesting research question is whether the analysis of social media content can result in identifying multiple complementary weak

G. Kalpakis · T. Tsikrika · I. Gialampoukidis · S. Papadopoulos · S. Vrochidis (✉)
I. Kompatsiaris
Information Technologies Institute, Centre for Research and Technology Hellas
Thermi-Thessaloniki, Thermi, Greece
e-mail: kalpakis@iti.gr; theodora.tsikrika@iti.gr; heliasgj@iti.gr; papadop@iti.gr; stefanos@iti.gr; ikom@iti.gr

© The Author(s) 2018
G. Leventakis, M. R. Haberfeld (eds.), *Community-Oriented Policing and Technological Innovations*, SpringerBriefs in Criminology,
https://doi.org/10.1007/978-3-319-89294-8_11

signals revealing the distinctive nature of terrorism-related content, and thus be an additional means towards the automatic or semi-automatic detection and subsequent removal of such content.

In this context, this work aims at analyzing the particular traits of terrorism-related content published on Twitter, a popular channel among terrorist groups, with the goal to distinguish terrorism-related accounts from others. To this end, a dataset of terrorism-related content was collected from Twitter through searches based on terrorism-related keywords provided by domain experts. In our study, we analyzed several textual, spatial, temporal and social network features of the gathered posts and their metadata and compared them against "neutral" Twitter content.

Our study unveiled a number of distinct characteristics of extremism and terrorism-related Twitter accounts and paves the path towards the development of automated tools that aim at leveraging the distinct traits of terrorism-related accounts for the early detection of terrorist and extremist content in Twitter, with the goal of alerting social media companies about the presence of such posts and speeding up the process of removing them from their platforms. This work is particularly timely given the recent pledges both by major social media platforms and governments around the world to step up their efforts towards countering online abusive content (Twitter Public Policy 2017).

Section "Related Work" summarizes related work in the area. Section "Data Collection and Analysis" describes the methodology and the dataset collected for our analysis. Section "Experimental Results" presents the findings of our analysis. Finally, Section "Conclusions" concludes with an outline of future research directions.

Related Work

Related research conducted in the past years has focused on examining the nature of terrorism-related content published by participants in extremist Web forums. Specifically, several research efforts have proposed methods for analyzing extremist Web forums for detecting users representing potential lone wolf terrorists and perpetrators of radical violence (Johansson et al. 2013; Scanlon and Gerber 2014). Additionally, the use of social media by terrorist and extremist groups and the resulting social network perspectives have also been studied. Recent works have examined the use of social media platforms by terrorist groups and organizations (Chatfield et al. 2015; Klausen 2015). Moreover, key player and key community identification in terrorism-related Twitter networks has been addressed through the use of different centrality measures and community detection algorithms (Gialampoukidis et al. 2016, 2017). Complementary to the aforementioned research efforts, our paper analyzes several textual, spatial, temporal and social network features which, when combined, are capable of characterizing the terrorism-related nature of Twitter accounts.

Data Collection and Analysis

Methodology

Our investigation focused on the Twitter platform given its popularity among terrorist groups as a means for spreading their propaganda and recruiting new members (Klausen 2015). Under the pressure put during the recent years by governments around the world to combat online extremism, Twitter has made significant efforts towards blocking accounts that promote terrorism and violence (Twitter Inc. 2016). In particular, Twitter has been suspending user accounts based on whether they are exhibiting abusive behavior that violates its rules,[1] including posting content related to violent threats, hate speech, and terrorism. To this end, Twitter has suspended 636,000 accounts between August 2015 and December 2016, with more than half of them occurring in the last 6 months of 2016 (Larson 2017).

In this context, we consider that Twitter accounts that have been posting content related to terrorism and are suspended at some point in time represent in principle users who have been exploiting the social media platform for serving their subversive intentions and promoting terrorism in general, e.g., disseminating propaganda, etc. Twitter accounts that have been posting content related to terrorism and have not been suspended are generally considered as users interested in the domain (e.g., posting news related to terrorism attacks), but without subversive intentions. There may of course be cases where non-suspended users also have darker motives and are actively engaging in propaganda and radicalization efforts, but have not thus far been detected so that they can be suspended by Twitter. In this work, we consider that this phenomenon might occur indeed but that it is less likely given Twitter's efforts in this direction.

Our analysis is based on the comparison of various characteristics of suspended Twitter accounts against those of non-suspended accounts. Both types of account post content relevant to the terrorism domain. The goal of our study is to determine the key factors that are capable of providing weak signals for distinguishing among ordinary Twitter users and those with subversive behavior based on the analysis of a variety of textual, spatial, temporal and social network features. The comparison is performed by examining the lifetime of suspended accounts, analyzing user accounts from the social network perspective (i.e. based on their connectivity with other user accounts), and exploiting geolocation information extracted from the textual content of user posts.

---

[1]https://support.twitter.com/articles/1831

Data Collection

The data for our study were collected using a social media crawling tool (Schinas et al. 2017) capable of running queries on the Twitter API[2] based on a set of five Arabic keywords related to terrorism propaganda. These keywords were provided by law enforcement agents and domain experts in the context of the activities of the EC-funded H2020 TENSOR[3] project and are related to the Caliphate, its news, publications and photos from the Caliphate area.

The crawling tool ran for a 7-month period, and specifically from February 9 to September 8, 2017, collecting tweets relevant to the provided keywords, along with information about the user accounts that published this content. Our dataset consists of 60,519 tweets posted by 33,827 Twitter users, with 4,967 accounts (14.70%) having been suspended by Twitter within this period.

For each tweet in our dataset, we stored its textual content together with relevant metadata, such as its URL address, the language used, its creation date, and the number of likes, shares, comments, and views. Similarly, for each user account having posted at least one tweet within our collection, we have captured its name, username, and creation date along with the number of its friends, followers, items (i.e. the total number of posts), favorites, and public lists that they are a member of.

Additionally, each user account was monitored on a daily basis to determine whether it has been suspended by Twitter. Given that Twitter does not provide information regarding the exact suspension date and time, this was determined based on the latest post published by a suspended account. Finally, after processing the data gathered, we built a social network graph representing the connectivity among Twitter accounts based on user mentions.

Experimental Results

This section presents the findings of our comparison between the suspended and non-suspended Twitter accounts on our dataset.

User Account Lifetime

First, we discuss the suspended Twitter account lifetime (see Fig. 11.1). Their lifetime is determined by computing the difference between the suspension date and the creation date of an account. The majority of suspended accounts (61.26%)

---

[2]https://dev.twitter.com/

[3]http://tensor-project.eu/

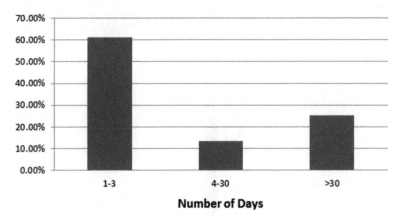

Fig. 11.1 Lifetime of suspended accounts

have very short lifetime, fluctuating between 1 and 3 days, which is explained by the efforts put by Twitter towards removing extremist content the moment it is posted. However, an interesting finding is that a significant portion of the suspended accounts (25.35%) have a lifetime longer than 30 days, which indicates that some accounts manage to evade the monitoring processes of Twitter for longer periods.

Analysis of Mention Networks

The analysis of mention networks formed by users in our dataset provides insights to the comparison between suspended and non-suspended accounts. The connectivity for the two account types differs with respect to the interconnection of accounts of the same type. In particular, 42.22% of the suspended accounts mention other suspended users, whereas 52.66% mention non-suspended accounts (the remaining 5.12% of the suspended accounts mention users are not included in our dataset and hence their suspension status is unknown). On the contrary, only 2.67% of non-suspended accounts mention suspended users, whereas 89.91% are connected with non-suspended users; again, the remaining 7.42% mention users not included in the dataset. This behavior reveals a community-like behavior, where accounts of the same type work together to fulfill their goals.

The connectivity pattern observed on the mention network is illustrated in the suspended to non-suspended mention ratio plot (see Fig. 11.2). The peak observed for mention ratio values fluctuating between 1 and 1.5 in the graph referring to suspended accounts indicates that a significant part of the them is connected to a larger number of suspended than non-suspended accounts, despite the fact that the vast majority of accounts gathered in our dataset are non-suspended users.

Fig. 11.2 Suspended to
non-suspended mention ratio

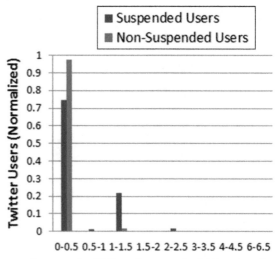

Fig. 11.3 Twitter account
friends

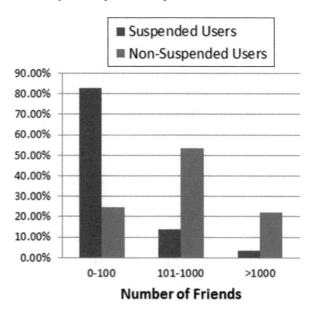

Friends and Followers

Figures 11.3 and 11.4 illustrate the distribution of numbers of friends and followers
per account type, respectively. In both cases, the vast majority of suspended users
have less than 100 friends or followers, which comes in contrast with the connectivity of non-suspended accounts. The short lifetime of terrorism-related accounts
(due to their suspension by Twitter) could be a determining factor regarding their
number of connections.

Fig. 11.4 Twitter account followers

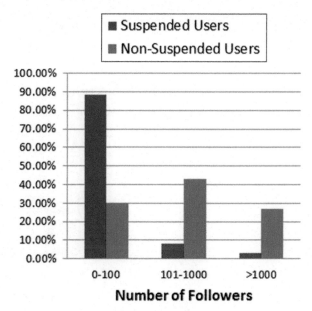

Fig. 11.5 Twitter account posts

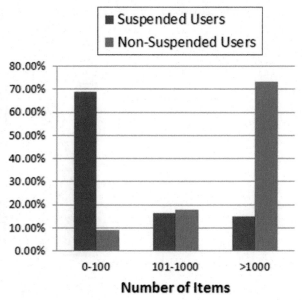

Posts, Favorites, and Lists

A similar trend is observed regarding the number of posted items and favorites per account type (see Figs. 11.5 and 11.6, respectively). The number of posts and favorites for the majority of suspended users is less than 100, whereas non-suspended accounts exhibit the inverse behavior.

Fig. 11.6 Twitter account favorites

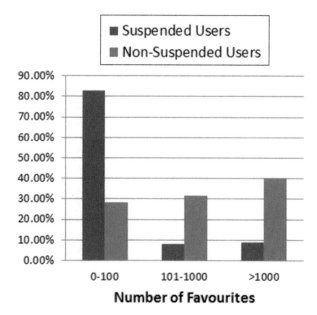

Fig. 11.7 Twitter account post rate

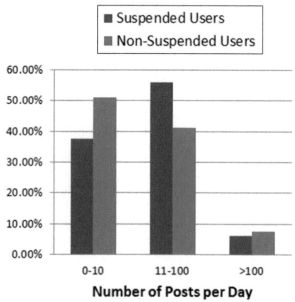

On the other hand, a different behavior is observed regarding the post rate (i.e. the number of posts per day) per account type (see Fig. 11.7). The majority of suspended accounts exhibit a post rate between 11 and 100 posts per day, whereas more than half of ordinary Twitter accounts post less than 10 tweets per day. This indicates that

Fig. 11.8 Number of times
listed

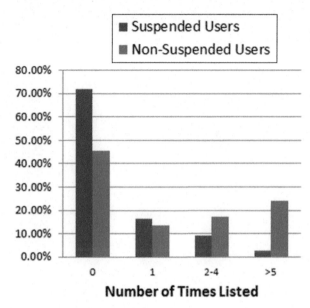

during their short lifetime, suspended accounts tend to post a relatively large number of tweets, possibly in an effort to disseminate many different pieces of information for spreading their propaganda.

Significant differences are also observed with respect to the number of public lists an account is a member of (see Fig. 11.8). The vast majority of suspended accounts (71.89%) are not a member in any list, whereas more than half of the non-suspended users are part of at least one list (54.48%), with almost one quarter of ordinary Twitter accounts being members in more than five lists.

Spatial Distribution of Accounts

To delve into the spatial distribution of accounts, we performed text-based analysis of the textual content of Twitter posts. We inferred the location of posts, even in cases when it was not explicitly available through the geotagging metadata accompanying a tweet. Geolocation inference from text was based on the approach by Kordopatis-Zilos et al. (2017), which employs refined language models learned from massive corpora of social media annotations. The results of the geolocation extraction for the posts of suspended and non-suspended users are presented in Figs. 11.9 and 11.10 respectively. Given that our dataset is retrieved based on a set of Arabic keywords, the geolocation information extracted for posts produced by both account types refers to countries from the Middle East and Northern Africa, whereas posts coming either from the United Arab Emirates or Syria are mostly associated with suspended accounts.

Fig. 11.9 Inferred locations from posts by suspended Twitter accounts

Fig. 11.10 Inferred locations from posts by non-suspended Twitter accounts

Conclusions

This paper aimed at understanding terrorism-related content on social media given their increasing employment by terrorist organizations for spreading their propaganda. We conducted an analysis on terrorism-related content posted on Twitter focusing on the differences between suspended and non-suspended accounts. Our analysis suggests that the traits observed in suspended users are different from non-suspended ones from several different perspectives, namely textual, spatial, temporal and social network features. These findings have the potential to set the basis for automated methods that detect accounts that are likely associated with abusive terrorism-related behavior. To this end, future work includes a more in-depth and large-scale analysis of features presented here, as well as taking into account additional features, including multimedia content such as images and videos.

Acknowledgements This work was supported by the TENSOR project (H2020-700024), funded by the European Commission.

References

Chatfield, A. T., Reddick, C. G., & Brajawidagda, U. (2015). Tweeting propaganda, radicalization and recruitment: Islamic state supporters multi-sided twitter networks. In *Proceedings of the 16th Annual International Conference on Digital Government Research* (pp. 239–249).

Gialampoukidis, I., Kalpakis, G., Tsikrika, T., Vrochidis, S., & Kompatsiaris, I. (2016). Key player identification in terrorism-related social media networks using centrality measures. In *Intelligence and Security Informatics Conference (EISIC), 2016 European* (pp. 112–115).

Gialampoukidis, I., Kalpakis, G., Tsikrika, T., Papadopoulos, S., Vrochidis, S., & Kompatsiaris, I. (2017). Detection of terrorism-related twitter communities using centrality scores. In *Proceedings of the 2nd International Workshop on Multimedia Forensics and Security* (pp. 21–25).

Johansson, F., Kaati, L., & Shrestha, A. (2013). Detecting multiple aliases in social media. In *Proceedings of the 2013 IEEE/ACM International Conference on Advances in Social Networks Analysis and Mining* (pp. 1004–1011).

Klausen, J. (2015). Tweeting the Jihad: Social media networks of western foreign fighters in Syria and Iraq. *Studies in Conflict & Terrorism, 38*(1), 1–22.

Kordopatis-Zilos, G., Papadopoulos, S., & Kompatsiaris, I. (2017). Geotagging text content with language models and feature mining. In *Proceedings of the IEEE*.

Larson S. (2017). *Twitter suspends 377,000 accounts for pro-terrorism content.*http:// money.cnn.com/2017/03/21/technology/twitter-bans-terrorism-accounts/index.html. Accessed 15 Sept 2017.

Scanlon, J. R., & Gerber, M. S. (2014). Automatic detection of cyber-recruitment by violent extremists. *Security Informatics, 3*(1), 5.

Schinas, M., Papadopoulos, S., Apostolidis, L., Kompatsiaris, Y., & Pericles, M. (2017). Open-source monitoring, search and analytics over social media. In *Proceedings of Internet Science Conference.* Springer.

Twitter Inc. (2016). *Combating violent extremism.*https://blog.twitter.com/official/en_us/a/2016/combating-violent-extremism.html. Accessed 15 Sept 2017.

Twitter Public Policy. (2017). *Global internet forum to counter terrorism.*https://blog.twitter.com/official/en_us/topics/company/2017/Global-Internet-Forum-to-Counter-Terrorism.html. Accessed 15 Sept 2017.

Chapter 12
UAVs and Their Use in Servicing the Community

George Eftychidis, Ilias Gkotsis, Panayiotis Kolios, and Costas Peleties

Introduction

Unmanned Aircraft Systems are small aerial vehicles that can be flown by a pilot via a ground control system, or autonomously through use of an on-board computer, communication links and additional equipment that is necessary to operate safely. All these components together are jointly referred to as Unmanned Aircraft Systems (UAS). The term UAS is the official term used by the U.S. Federal Aviation Administration to describe such type of aircrafts. Unmanned defines that they fly with no human pilot on board, the term aircraft is used to comply with airworthiness and airspace regulations, and the term systems is used to emphasize the associated support equipment, control station, data links, telemetry, communications and navigation equipment, etc., necessary to operate the unmanned aircraft (Austin 2010). Other terms are also widely used to refer to these systems, such as Drones (Dynamic Remotely Operated Navigation Equipment), RPVs (Remotely Piloted Vehicles) and RPAS (Remotely Piloted Aircraft Systems) (Federal Aviation Administration).

The use of UAS has shown to be extremely beneficial in many situations and their popularity is increasing in a very fast pace, due to their great advantages over manned aircrafts. For example, UAS have lower cost of acquisition, operation

G. Eftychidis · I. Gkotsis (✉)
Centre for Security Studies, Athens, Greece
e-mail: g.eftychidis@kemea-research.gr; i.gkotsis@kemea-research.gr

P. Kolios
KIOS Research Center, University of Cyprus, Nicosia, Cyprus
e-mail: pkolios@ucy.ac.cy

C. Peleties
Cyprus Civil Defence, Nicosia, Cyprus

© The Author(s) 2018
G. Leventakis, M. R. Haberfeld (eds.), *Community-Oriented Policing and Technological Innovations*, SpringerBriefs in Criminology,
https://doi.org/10.1007/978-3-319-89294-8_12

119

and maintenance, have longer operational endurance, need reduced pilot skills and can be operated with minimum human intervention and, depending on the system, they can operate even for hours under difficult conditions, without loss of concentration and fatigue. Moreover, UAS can be deployed in a variety of terrains and harsh environments, can access hazardous sites and contaminated spaces which are dangerous for flight crews onboard, and can perform visual or thermal imaging of an affected area (Deliverable 61.2 Position Paper).

Undoubtedly, all these features can prove extremely beneficial to civil protection missions (covering both prevention and preparedness), having though an impact on the performance of the UAS in terms of operational times and overall time management. In frame of PREDICATE project, we seek to integrate UAS capabilities to the specific civil protection needs aiming to increase operational effectiveness and decrease operational costs; while decreasing the response time required in disaster prevention and emergency response missions. It is evident that, the sooner a victim of an unlawful act or a missing person during search and rescue is located by law enforcement or civil protection services, the sooner protection and medical aid will be offered and the better the chances of release and survival. Furthermore, AS can support first responder operations and may increase situational awareness of civil protection agencies.

UAS vary greatly in size, flying capability, capacity and methods of control. Nowadays, UAS are used in many parts of Europe to monitor roads, railway systems and infrastructure, to survey agricultural production, to enhance the capabilities of commercial photography, to support wide area mapping and surveillance, to check on wind turbines, electricity pylons, dams and other elements and networks of critical infrastructures. In Fig. 12.1 below, the major categories of UAS civilian application fields are depicted. The capabilities of UAS pave their way to developing civilian applications associated to Community policing within the category of Homeland Security.

Needs Assessment

UAS and in particular rotorcrafts can offer many beneficial support services to civil protection and community policing activities in a variety of ways. Broadly speaking, these services can be classified in two categories, based on their relative purpose of use. They can either deliver help (helper) or provide observation/information (informer/observer). A helper UAS can be used to support civil protection response operations by shipping important dispensable equipment payloads quickly and effectively (i.e. shipping equipment such as a life vest, a defibrillator, a first-aid kit, a thermal blanket, water and food, etc.). An observer UAS can be used to maximize situational awareness and support the personnel of civil protection organizations and community policing organizations in deciding or planning their actions during field operations (i.e. monitor the evolution of field operations or state of unlawful acts,

Civilian Application Fields for UAS

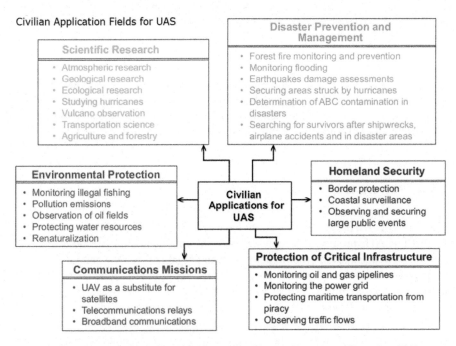

Fig. 12.1 Civilian applications for UAS (diagram by Therese Skrzypietz) (Skrzypietz 2012).

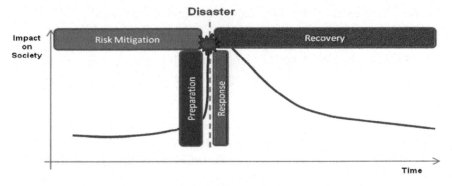

Fig. 12.2 Timeline of effects of a disaster (Deliverable 61.2 Position Paper)

identify threats or evaluate particular situations). The presence or appearance of a UAS may have also deterrent effects in the evolution of an illegal action.

In case of disasters, the public sector is often paralyzed due to eventual damages to infrastructures and disruption of critical services. Figure 12.2 illustrates a natural disaster timeline, with its changing impacts, over four stages: (Risk Mitigation, Preparation, Response, and Recovery). The area beneath the red time-line represents the impact on society, and includes: casualties, negative impact on livelihoods, and, depending on the socio-economic resilience capacity, regression in development.

Time is a crucial factor during emergencies and any unexpected situation. Hence rapidly available and highly deployable equipment is directly linked with response efficiency and mission performance. In that respect, UAS platforms provide an increase in operational effectiveness; while at the same time they decrease operational costs and operational response time. The public emergency services and law enforcement agencies shall potentially use the UAS technology in a variety of ways, depending on the phase of the operations, the level of risk or incident and the type of UAS being used (European Emergency Number Association – EENA 112 2016).

Civil Protection Operational Needs

The needs of civil protection operations have been discussed and elaborated in frame of PREDICATE project with representatives of emergency organizations and law enforcement agencies in order to determine and organize the relevant requirements aiming to address the respective needs. The information was enriched through an extensive literature review, properly prepared questionnaires, physical meetings and personal interviews with relevant experts and representatives of public agencies in Greece and Cyprus. Based on the feedback received during the aforementioned knowledge elicitation activity, the civil protection operations that can be supported, exploiting the UAS capabilities are arranged into four main groups as follows:

- The Reconnaissance And Mapping (RAM) group, refers to the use of UAS platforms and their respective payloads in order to identify and locate vulnerabilities, hazards, and threats that may evolve to natural/man-made/technological emergencies (Se et al. 2009). In addition, RAM is related with the detection and assessment of changes over large Regions of Interest (RoI) and the mapping of such changes to inform prevention plans. The RAM group of operations can be associated with the management of risks and disasters at all levels of the command chain, supporting public actors involved in civil protection tasks with consistent surveillance of large areas, timely risk identification and informed decision making on a concrete situation. The Monitoring and Tracking (MAT) group of operations, refers to the process of persistent surveillance of Areas of Interest (areas smaller than RoIs), stricken by specific emergencies (American Red Cross and Measure 2015). In such situations Search and Rescue (SaR), live saving and evacuation are the primary tasks for the civil protection personnel. MAT is a dynamic process at the operational and tactical level that offers valuable input for deciding response actions and first responders' operations as well as for leveraging situation awareness in crisis management by enriching situational crisis picture. In terms of community policing tasks this type of operations can be combined with monitoring of events in open public spaces involving large crowds, confirmation of unlawful activity in public safety situations etc.
- The group of Temporary Utility Infrastructure (TUI) operations is relative to the task of offering an alternative utility infrastructure, using UAS. Examples of TUI

operations include primarily telecommunication services (Li et al. 2016) e.g. UAS acting as a relay radio communication node, for illuminating dark areas during the night (Direct Line for Business 2017), as notice boards to display inform and replaying of acoustic messages. Multiple drones may be deployed in swarms, e.g., to map out and track pollution or to make up a grid network and relay the data over large distances (White et al. 2008).

- Delivery of Help-Aid (DOH), refers to the process of delivering or releasing (after adjusting custom made equipment, such us buckets, claws, etc.) urgent medical and other supplies to those in need, including: first-aid kits (QuiQui-automated drone delivery of pharmacy items), tools, bottles of water, blood, defibrillators, medications or other healthcare items (Scott and Scott 2017). Delivery method can use automated ground station, parachute, rope dropping, ground landing etc. Thus, despite issues related to privacy, security, safety and regulation need to be addressed, UAS can provide beneficial and ubiquitous support to civil protection, law enforcement and healthcare emergencies.

Community Policing Operational Needs

In accordance to the civil protection operational needs and extended to community policing purposes, there are many applications for the employment of unmanned systems for law enforcement. UAS are able to enhance situational awareness and force protection of officers in the field. Examples include over-watch of vehicle checkpoint and search, situational awareness during hostage situations (close look through windows without risk), traffic monitoring, neighbourhood watch, petty crime response, suspect monitoring, patrolling, incident reconstruction, assistance in vehicle apprehension, crowd monitoring and control (using loudspeakers), disaster response and management, wide area detection of drug making facilities, drug crop detection, distributed video to ground patrols and HQ facilities simultaneously (Fig. 12.3).

UAS have the potential to improve both community and officer safety, while decreasing the cost of improved operations. Some indicative cases are the following (Valdovinos et al. 2016):

- Search and Rescue Operations: a UAS is able to maneuver in relatively small and difficult-to-access areas in order to locate individuals with special needs or disabilities.
- Protecting Officer Safety: Some departments use UAS to get a better look at suspicious packages or locate hidden (and possibly dangerous) suspects while reducing risk to officers.
- Helping Police to respond to criminal actions: Rapid assessment of field conditions and situational awareness that can support intervention and planning.
- Accident and Crime Scene Investigations: An aerial survey by a UAS, particularly one equipped with GIS mapping software, can save hours in follow-up

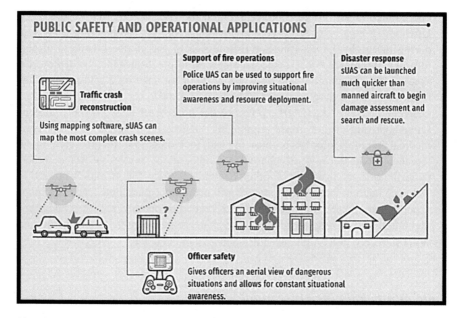

Fig. 12.3 Public safety and civilian applications of UAS

investigations. This can speed up accident and crime scene investigation and report preparation and may reduce incidental traffic associated with a scene investigation.

- Disaster Management: UAS can survey damage in flooded or inaccessible areas quickly, saving responders vital time and protecting their safety.
- Perimeter Security: UAS can provide views of hard-to-access areas, improving officer and public safety. This can be crucial in securing areas before public events as well as in border protection.
- Active Pursuit Support: Focus group members noted that using UAS to follow fleeing suspects, particularly when they are on foot, protects officer safety, and could also reduce the danger to the public.
- Monitor waste disposal and other environmental crimes: Activation of UAS following citizens' complaints.
- Support and Coordination with Fire/EMS and Other Government Agencies: Firefighter safety could be greatly improved by the use of a UAS to view roof damage during a fire. Additionally, public works, community development, parks and recreation, environmental work (such as mosquito control), transportation (like mapping evacuation routes), planning, and many other public responsibilities could benefit from implementation of UAS technology.

It has to be noticed that, in context of community policing, the operator of UAS can be a private pilot, member of a local community, or Police department linked to organized communities of citizens. In all cases the legal restrictions and constraints for using UAS in urban environment should be considered. In case of PREDICATE, the cooperation with Cyprus Civil Defence included the option of civil protection volunteers as community actors who are authorized to use UAS for operational purposes, including situational awareness and search and rescue.

UAS Capabilities and Operational Requirements

UAS Component Categories and Types

The category and type of available components are the factors that define the operational capabilities of an assembled UAS platform. These capabilities include the air-cruise speed, the altitude and autonomy of the flight, the deploy ability, the performance to environmental conditions, hovering, manoeuvrability, range and endurance, communications range and the size of the platform. It is thus important for UAS users to know which are the categories and the types of available components that they can consider for designing a system, which can address their respective operational needs. The PREDICATE project considers both fixed-wing UAV and rotor crafts (VTOL). Fixed-wing are more efficient regarding endurance and payload while rotor crafts are comparatively more agile and fault tolerant. An overview of the respective performance and specifications of currently available in the market UAS is shown in Fig. 12.4.

Community policing solutions need to consider rather Small UAS and rotor crafts than fixed-wing UAS.

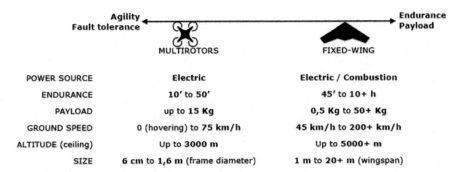

	MULTIROTORS	FIXED-WING
POWER SOURCE	Electric	Electric / Combustion
ENDURANCE	10' to 50'	45' to 10+ h
PAYLOAD	up to 15 Kg	0,5 Kg to 50+ Kg
GROUND SPEED	0 (hovering) to 75 km/h	45 km/h to 200+ km/h
ALTITUDE (ceiling)	Up to 3000 m	Up to 5000+ m
SIZE	6 cm to 1,6 m (frame diameter)	1 m to 20+ m (wingspan)

Fig. 12.4 Average commercial UAS specs & performance (European Emergency Number Association – EENA 112 2016)

Table 12.1 PREDICATE needs' assessment matrix for civil protection operations

		Operational need				
		Reconnaissance and mapping (RAM)	Monitoring and tracking (MAT)	Temporary utility infrastructure (TUI)	Delivery of help-aid (DOH)	Overall rating score
UAS capabilities	Carry heavy payload	3	2	5	4	3
	Deploy ability	4	5	5	5	5
	Ease-of-use	5	5	5	5	5
	High airspeed	3	3	1	2	2
	High altitude	3	1	2	1	2
	Hovering	2	2	5	5	3
	Long endurance	4	5	5	5	5
	Long range	3	3	2	3	3
	Maneuverability	3	3	3	3	3

Operational Requirements

A number of technical specifications is required by UAS in order to address the needs of civil protection operations. Nine UAS capabilities have been defined in PREDICATE in order to organize and formalize the ability of the system to perform particular missions and support specific type of operations. These capabilities according to their ratings are depicted in Table 12.1.

High deploy-ability is essential, since response operations require prompt reaction and minimal pre-flight preparation. Thus, UAS platforms should have quick and adaptive deployment ability to ensure they can be deployed quickly even in challenging terrain (e.g. ruined buildings, burned areas, tight spaces).

One particular advantage of the microdrones UAS is the ease with which they can be used. It takes only a short time to learn how to fly and steer these aerial platforms (either in manual or automatic mode), thereby saving on costly training programs. This is crucial for civil protection organizations, the personnel of which are usually volunteers with no previous aviation background or knowledge. Although UAS pilot training for civil protection operations is obligatory the easiness of use is important for introducing UAS in operational tasks and for increasing the efficiency of the operations. Easiness of use in context of civil protection operations is directly related with the hovering ability of UAS and in particular of rotorcrafts. Hovering allows the operator to monitor an event and take unique viewing angles easy and effectively, while the UAS will stay in a specific position as much is required. Endurance is another technical specification which is quite important for civil protection operations. It is obvious that longer endurance provides higher performance as well as lower costs in terms of extra recharging/replacement components. Other UAS capabilities such as long-range flight, manoeuvrability and increased payload capacity[1] have been considered as features of medium importance in civil protection operations. Carrying a heavy payload could be beneficial for some operations, especially when delivering equipment. High speed and high-altitude requirements are not considered important for civil protection UAS missions. In context of PREDICATE, a number of DJI UAS solutions (Matrice 100, Matrice 600 and S1000) was used, which have payload capacity between 3 and 7 kgs, flight time (with payload) between 15′ and 40′ and control range spanning up to 5 km. A number of these UAS was used by the Cyprus Civil Defence for validating the performance of PREDICATE system for operational purposes.

Mission Planning

Visual Data Gathering

Cameras are the primary instruments used on-board of UAS for supporting disaster prevention and perform emergency response missions. They are usually optical sensors operating on the visible light spectrum or infrared, operating in low-light conditions and detecting emitted heat. Visual cameras can directly provide information from the incident field or a region of interest in the form of real-time images and video streams. The procedure of visual data collection is vital in criticality assessment, search and rescue, and monitoring type of missions. Key to visual data collection is the ability of discriminating between objects of interest, where the task is to locate all instances of an object of interest in the captured imagery data.

In order to perform accurate visual analysis (i.e. identifying all objects/areas of interest correctly, without false positive/negative detections), the camera resolution has to be adequate in order to apply Johnson's criteria for defining the number of picture elements (pixels) required to discriminate an object on an image, based on three main levels with more than 50% probability of success (Waharte and Trigoni 2010; Kopeika 1998; TREC 2016). The three levels of discrimination are detection, recognition and identification as shown in Fig. 12.5, which illustrates the relative results achieved in terms of picture elements.

The distance of the camera sensor from the target affects the image resolution and therefore the flight altitude of a UAS carrying the camera is also affected. This means that in order to ensure higher resolution the UAS should fly in lower altitudes. However, flying at lower altitudes will have an impact on the flight performance, since the ground FOV of the camera will become narrower, which fact will lead to longer flight times for the same ROI. The discrimination level should provide enough information for the particular mission while maintaining a feasible and

---

[1] A payload is the cargo or equipment a UAS carries that is not required for flight, control and navigation. Payload is a percentage of the total take-off weight of the vehicle.

Detection   Identification   Recognition

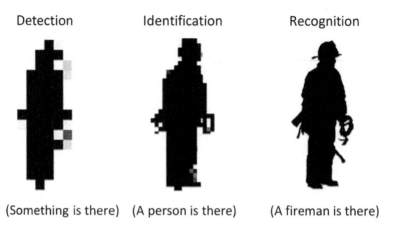

(Something is there)   (A person is there)   (A fireman is there)

Fig. 12.5 Johnson's criteria discrimination levels (UVSS – United Vision Security Systems 2016)

useful flight plan, eliminating eventual false positives/negatives (UAV Vision 2016). For civil protection, target (object) recognition and tracking is considered the most important task.

Heat sources such as humans, animals, cars etc. can be detected and recognized using infrared cameras. In the respective images, hot objects are coloured white while less warm or cold objects are coloured darker or black. The imagerycollectedcanbeprocessedlocallybyacomputersystemon-boardthe UAS in order to enhance the image, detect and recognize specific objects; or it can be sent to remote control centres for post-processing.

Path Planning

Path planning is the final outcome of PREDICATE project, which provides an up-loadable flight plan to the UAS, based on the mission data calculated using the relative user inputs. It is assumed that for any type of mission, the region of interest that will be scanned is known a priori and segmented into a number of (N) tiles, which the UAS has to sweep, covering all segments before completing its mission. The operational time is governed primarily by the selection of the platform and the payload that will be used.

For the path planning purposes, a tool (Fig. 12.6) has been developed during PREDICATE, specifically for Android devices, providing an easy and organized graphical interface and advanced automated capacities for the end users, such as automatic flight, object tracking, picture stitching and several other capabilities.

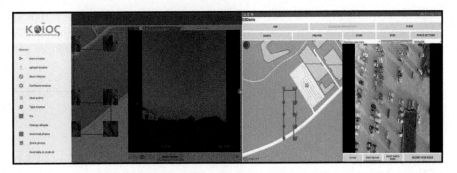

Fig. 12.6 PREDICATE mission planning toolkit

Fig. 12.7 Mapping and reconnaissance (left), monitoring and tracking (center) and temporary utility infrastructure (right) operations

Proof of Concept

As stated above, UAS can be of benefit for a number of emergency management and public safety applications. This has been validated and demonstrated through several field tests, exercises and activities where PREDICATE participated officially.[2] These events provided the opportunity to test the performance of the system in a variety of mission types as regards mapping, monitoring and infrastructure provision during emergencies (Fig. 12.7). The integration of PREDICATE functionality in community policing tasks has been tested in context of the demonstrations performed during the NGCP International conference on community policing held in Heraklion, Crete (Gr) in October 2017.[3] In this case, PREDICATE mission was linked to the back-end system of INSPEC[2]T[4] and fed with the coordinates of the

---

[2]http://www.kios.ucy.ac.cy/predicate/index.php/photos/category/34

[3]http://ngcpconference.com/

[4]http://www.inspec2t-project.eu/

incident site to monitor. The PREDICATE UAS received the coordinates of Points of Interest from the INSPEC^{2}T system, plan the respective path and automatically take-off and fly to the site providing the control center with real time images and video streaming from the incident place.

Conclusions

This paper provides an update on the results of the PREDICATE project of DG ECHO and focuses to the possible extension of the use of UAS for improving public safety based on the strengthening of community policing capabilities. As described in the above sections, one of the major outcomes of the project is a mission and path planning utility, which can be uploaded by community policing control centers to a variety of UAS and allow them to perform mission specific flights over specific sites of interest. Using the developments of PREDICATE and the appropriate payloads the UAS can be used for scanning the region for search and rescue purposes, aiming to detect, recognize and identify missing persons and abandoned objects, persons in trouble due to criminal activity or entrapped people.

Such tools (as of PREDICATE) and UAS (especially small ones such as quadcopters) can be a great asset either for civil protection or law enforcement agencies, while serving the community. The aforementioned capabilities can provide improved operational preparedness, reduced response time and increased information and data flow from the incident scene, combined also with the ability of automatic mission deployment. The burst of the UAS market and their use by volunteers and hobbyists can be exploited in context of community policing for strengthening the efficiency of law enforcement in a continuously threatened European society.

It must be considered though by the operating authorities, that procedural justice, transparency, and accountability should be maintained, and that they are responsible of balancing the benefits of such technologies with the preservation of community privacy, safety, and other concerns.

Acknowledgments This work has been partially funded from the European Union's Humanitarian Aid and Civil Protection project "PREDICATE" under grant agreement ECHO/SUB/2015/713851/PREV29.

References

American Red Cross and Measure. (2015). *Drones for disaster response and relief operations.* https://www.issuelab.org/resources/21683/21683.pdf
Austin, R. (2010). *Unmanned aircraft systems: UAVS design, development and deployment.* Chichester: Wiley.

Deliverable 61.2 Position Paper. The future of UAVs for civil security applications, AIRBEAM Project (261769).

Direct Line for Business. (2017, March). https://www.directline.com/lib/campaign/fleetlights/pdf/fleetlights_tech_manual.pdf

European Emergency Number Association – EENA 112. (2016). *EENA operations document – RPAS and the emergency services*. www.eena.org/download.asp?item_id=153

Federal Aviation Administration. *Frequently asked questions/help*. https://www.faa.gov/uas/faqs/. Accessed 10 Apr 2016.

Kopeika, N. S. (1998). *A system engineering approach to imaging*. Bellingham: SPIE Optical Engineering Press.

Li, B., Jiang, Y., Sun, J., Cai, L., & Wen, C.-Y. (2016). Development and testing of a two-UAV communication relay system. *Sensors, 16*, 1696.

QuiQui-automated drone delivery of pharmacy items. http://quiqui.me/

Scott, J., & Scott, C. (2017). Drone delivery models for healthcare. In *Proceedings of the 50th Hawaii International Conference on System Sciences, HICSS*.

Se, S., Firoozfam, P., Goldstein, N., Wu, L., Dutkiewicz, M., et al. (2009). Automated UAV-based mapping for airborne reconnaissance and video exploitation. In *Proceedings of SPIE 7307, Airborne Intelligence, Surveillance, Reconnaissance (ISR) Systems and Applications VI*, 73070M.

Skrzypietz, T. (2012, February). *Unmanned aircraft systems for civilian mission*. Brandenburg Institute for Society and Security (BIGS) Policy Paper.

TREC. (2016). *Johnson's criteria for pixel resolution: Four levels of discrimination*. http://www.trec.com/johnsoncriteria.html. Accessed 16 Nov 2016.

UAV Vision. (2016). *A practical explanation of the Johnson criteria*. http://www.uavvision.com/news/practical-explanation-johnson-criteria. Accessed 12 May 2016.

UVSS – United Vision Security Systems. (2016). *We specialize in long range camera*. http://ev3000.com/uvss-llc/Home.html. Accessed 16 Nov 2016.

Valdovinos, M., Specht, J., & Zeunik, J. (2016). *Law enforcement & Unmanned Aircraft Systems (UAS): Guidelines to enhance community trust*. Washington, DC: Office of Community Oriented Policing Services.

Waharte, S., & Trigoni, N. (2010, September). Supporting search and rescue operations with UAVs. In *2010 International Conference on Emerging Security Technologies* (pp. 6–7). Canterbury.

White, B. A., Tsourdos, A., Ashokaraj, I., Subchan, S., & Zbikowski, R. (2008). Contaminant cloud boundary monitoring using network of UAV sensors. *IEEE Sensors Journal, 8*, 1681–1692.

Printed by Printforce, the Netherlands